Contents

Page

Illustrations

Chapter 1

Introduction

*It's politically sensitive, but it's going to happen. Some people don't want to hear this, and it sure isn't in vogue ... but—absolutely—we're going to fight **in** space. We're going to fight **from** space and we're going to fight **into** space...*

General Joseph W. Ashy
Former Commander in Chief U.S. Space Command

The world may be on the verge of a new era of warfare, one where battles are not fought only within the biosphere of the Earth, but also in the space surrounding it. Recent conflicts have shown the tremendous advantages conferred upon those who have the advantage of space-based assets, limited though they are to helping forces navigate, communicate and spy upon their enemies. Some argue that fighting in space itself is inevitable, while others hold that space should be maintained as a sanctuary, free of weapons. The purpose of this paper is not to argue for or against the weaponization of space, but rather to examine the kinds of weapons that have been proposed for use in space and compare their capabilities with those of their surface-based counterparts. In making this analysis, the efficacy of various concepts will be measured by balancing three measures: cost; technical feasibility; and each weapon's ability to provide the advantages of using space to the United States and her allies, or denying such advantages to an enemy.

The United States currently enjoys an overwhelming advantage in space-based surveillance, communications and navigation aids. Protecting these assets and maintaining U.S. dominance in space is potentially critical to the defense of U.S. national interests. As U.S. national space policy indicates, leaders at the highest levels of

1

government recognize this potential vulnerability. The policy explicitly states that national security space activities must deter, warn, and if necessary, defend against enemy attack. It also states that "DOD shall maintain the capability to execute the mission areas of … space control, and force application." Finally, current policy stipulates that "the United States will develop, operate and maintain space control capabilities to ensure freedom of action in space and, if directed, deny such freedom of action to adversaries."[1]

The leadership of the United States Air Force (USAF) supports this policy and believes that implementing it will almost inevitably require deploying weapons in space. This outlook is evident in numerous speeches and official statements. Even before General Ashy made the statement quoted above, USAF Vice Chief of Staff General Thomas S. Moorman Jr. said in a June 1996 speech:

> Undoubtedly the most provocative subject in any discussion of the future of space is the subject of space weapons and the likelihood of their use. Here I am referring to the broadest categories: Space-based lasers to shoot down hostile ICBMs, space weapons that attack other satellites, or weapons released from space platforms that destroy terrestrial targets. Today, these kinds of systems clearly break the current thresholds of acceptability ... But the 21st century could well see a change.[2]

This sentiment was echoed again by the commander in chief of U.S. Space Command, General Howell M. Estes III, in his comments to Congress: "Space remains on the cutting edge—support to our warfighter, even the potential for war itself, is moving from Earth into space."[3] This outlook will likely shape U.S. space initiatives in the immediate future.

The pressure toward weaponizing space received additional impetus in response to President Clinton's recent line-item veto of three space weapon-related programs: Clementine II, the Army Kinetic-Kill Anti-Satellite (ASAT) program, and the Military

---

[1] "Fact Sheet: National Space Policy," (Washington D.C.: The White House National Science and Technology Council, 1996), 1-6.
[2] General Thomas S. Moorman Jr., vice chief of staff, USAF, "The Challenges of Space Beyond 2000," Remarks to the 75th Royal Australian Air Force Anniversary Airpower Conference, Canberra, Australia, 14 June 1996; on-line, Internet, 9 January 1998, available from http://www.af mil/news/speech/current/The_Challenges_of_Space_Bey html
[3] Air Force General Howell M. Estes III, commander-in-chief, North American Aerospace Defense Command and U.S. Space Command; Prepared statement before the Senate Armed Services Committee, Washington D.C., 13 March 1997.

Space Plane. These cancellations prompted forty-three high-ranking retired military leaders to issue an open letter to the president urging him to change his decision. This letter refers to space-based missile defense and neutralizing enemy satellites as "missions the United States military must be prepared to perform."[4]

It is often assumed that defending space-based assets, and neutralizing weapons that make use of space, require the deployment of weapons *in* space. While space-based weapons should not be dismissed from consideration without a thorough evaluation, this evaluation appears to have been skipped in the technological push to develop space-based weapons. Major questions that have yet to be adequately addressed are: What do *space-based* weapons have to offer that other forms of military power lack? What are space-based weapons likely to cost, both in terms of dollars and in lost opportunities for pursuing other systems? A related concern is what capabilities these weapons will confer upon other nations if they eventually emulate a U.S. deployment. This paper attempts to address these questions and determine what space-based weapons can be expected to bring to the table. To begin, we will summarize the arguments on both sides of the space weaponization debate.

Arguments For Weaponizing Space

The arguments in favor of weaponizing space center around the fact that the United States relies heavily on space-based assets for both military and commercial needs. Protecting these assets will become increasingly important as access to space becomes cheaper and the technology needed for this access becomes more available. As General Estes said before Congress: "Increased reliance on space systems means improved capabilities, but also new vulnerabilities...The U.S. must be able to control the medium of space to assure our access and deny the same to any adversary."[5] Retired General "Mike" Loh, former commander of U.S. Air Combat Command, echoed this concern at a recent Center for Security Policy roundtable discussion titled "The Need for American Space Dominance." In outlining the U.S. dependence on space-based assets,

---

[4] James A. Abrahamson et al., open letter to President Clinton, dated 15 January 1998, included in The Center For Security Policy press release No. 98-P7, 15 January 1998.

General Loh noted that "It is almost frightening when you...look at how little we have allowed for the protection...of those assets."[6] While these statements do not explicitly call for space-based weapons to effect this control, a key underlying assumption of this argument is that space-based weapons are needed to do the job. As a consequence no restrictions should be placed on their development, testing, and eventual deployment.

Another line of argument in favor of space-based weapons, or at least an argument for why they are inevitable, devolves from the fact that every environment accessible to man has eventually become an arena for combat. This line of reasoning was noticeable in then-Secretary of the Air Force Sheila Widnall's address to the National Security Forum in May 1997:

> You have, first off, a fundamental question of whether we will place weapons in space. We have a lot of history that tells us that warfare migrates where it can—that nations engaged in a conflict do what they can, wherever they must. At a very tender age, aviation went from a peaceful sport, to a supporting function, very analogous to what we do today in space—to a combat arm. Our space forces may well follow that same path.[7]

This argument holds that the evolution of warfare will inevitably require placing weapons in space in order to fulfill a multitude of military roles. These roles include defending against ballistic missile attack, defending space-based assets (the space control mission), and attacking terrestrial targets (the force application mission).

Some take the argument a step further, believing that it is probably too late to head off the weaponization of space. Major General Dickman, the DOD Space Architect, made this argument in a 1997 Huntsville address:

> To hope that there will never be conflict in space is to ignore the past. As space access becomes routine, ... as national security becomes a matter of information dominance as well as other military strength, the risk-benefit

---

5 Ibid.
6 "Summary of The Center for Security Policy High-Level Roundtable Discussion of 'The Need for American Space Dominance'," attachment to The Center for Security Policy press release No. 98-16P, 23 January 1998, 5; on-line, Internet, 28 January 1998, available from http://www.security-policy.org/papers/98-P16at.html.
7 The Honorable Sheila E. Widnall, secretary of the Air Force, "The Space and Air Force of the Next Century," address to the National Security Forum, Maxwell Air Force Base, Ala., May 29, 1997; on-line, Internet, 9 January 1998, available from http://www.af.mil/news/speech/current/The_Space_and_Air_Force_of_.html

assessment for interfering with space capabilities will change. Tomorrow, space won't provide a sanctuary for systems that can provide a decisive edge in combat, any more than the air or the ocean depths do today. Tomorrow, commercial endeavors will look to the government for protection, as they have on land and at sea for over 200 years.[8]

The main contention of the argument is that space today is analogous to aviation prior to World War I. The transition of aviation from being a support service to being a combat arm will soon be emulated by space systems. Any attempt to thwart this process is not only doomed to fail; it will leave the United States vulnerable to attack from nations that aggressively pursue space weaponization.

Arguments Against Weaponizing Space

Today the United States is in an enviable position: it is the only nation on earth that can project non-nuclear combat power to anywhere on the globe. Never before has a single nation had such an uncontested ability to intervene in events around the world. However this capability comes at great expense. From long-endurance submarines to fleets of combat aircraft and their supporting tankers, the physical assets necessary to provide this capability are extensive and were only made possible by a sustained effort during the long years of the Cold War. In addition to the equipment, large numbers of military personnel require years of intensive training and continual practice in order to make the system work. With the demise of the Soviet Union, the United States is free to intervene anywhere that it chooses, so it would appear to be in the best interests of the United States to maintain the status quo.

In developing this world-spanning power projection capability, the United States has come to rely heavily on space-based assets for communication, navigation and surveillance. Protecting these capabilities, and denying an enemy similar ones, is essential if U.S. armed forces are to remain dominant on the battlefield. That doing this requires the development and deployment of space-based weapons does not necessarily

---

[8] Major General Robert Dickman, "The Evolution of Space Operations and Warfare," address to AIAA Symposium, Huntsville, Ala., September 23, 1997; on-line, Internet, 2 February 1998, available from http://www.acq.osd mil/space/architect/spcweb html.

follow; in fact, deploying space-based weapons is just as likely to place other space-based assets in jeopardy.[9] Indeed, the proliferation of space-based weapons may even give potential adversaries the ability to strike at the United States without incurring the enormous costs of U.S.-style armed forces.

If the United States develops and deploys space-based weapons for controlling space, self-interest dictates that other countries will follow suit. As with other technology, the greatest costs are normally incurred in the initial research and development required to evolve a concept into a weapon. Once a new weapon has been deployed it is much easier, and less expensive, to observe the operational system, determine how it must operate, and then duplicate it. By doing this initial research and development, the United States will be paving the way for other nations to follow. The result may well be that assets which are now safe, because no other nation has a pressing need to develop weapons to attack them, will become vulnerable to attack because other nations will feel compelled to emulate the United States and deploy space-based weapons of their own.

The argument against space-based weapons for attacking airborne or surface targets is very similar. If the United States deploys such weapons, other nations may feel compelled to do likewise. In this case, the United States would not only be making a segment of its defense system vulnerable to attack, we could very well make U.S. cities vulnerable. Unfriendly nations with orbital weapons capable of attacking terrestrial targets would be able to strike the United States, or anywhere else on the globe, without investing the tremendous resources necessary to field a U.S.-style military. This would, in effect, negate our present ability to intervene wherever it is in our interest to do so, since a country possessing these orbital weapons would be able to strike back. With the technology necessary to launch satellites even now becoming widely available, the number of countries capable of deploying space-based weapons is growing. This proliferation of technology makes U.S. development of space-based weapons fraught with peril.

---

[9] A thorough discussion of this point may be found in David W. Ziegler, *Safe Heavens: Military Strategy and Space Sanctuary Thought*, Master's thesis, School of Advanced Airpower Studies, June 1997.

In consideration of the arguments outlined above, it seems to be much more in the interest of the United States to advocate a treaty banning space-based weapons entirely. Given the current international climate of antipathy toward weaponizing space, such a treaty is entirely plausible. Admittedly, space-based weapons are probably inevitable in the long term, however their eventual deployment can probably be delayed for decades, if not longer, with a carefully written treaty.

Thesis Overview

As is evident in the preceding summaries, arguments have traditionally focused on why weapons should, or should not, be deployed in space. These arguments typically ignore questions about exactly what space-based weapons can do that more conventional weapons are unable to do, or can only accomplish at great cost. Any decision about placing weapons in space, either for or against, should be based on a firm foundation of knowledge about what these weapons are, how much they are likely to cost, and what other options are available for accomplishing the same missions. The purpose of this paper is to evaluate proposed space-based weapons and compare them with their terrestrial counterparts so that an informed decision about weaponizing space can be made.

The concepts discussed in this paper are based on open-source documentation of space weapon concepts currently being pursued or under consideration. The nature of these weapons is such that many of them can be used for more than one purpose. In an attempt to construct a logical and easily understood analysis, the types of weapons and their capabilities are discussed in several chapters. Chapter 2 will lay out the concepts for space-based weapons that have been proposed, their expected capabilities and the technological risks involved in pursuing them. Chapter 3 will focus on alternatives to space-based weapons that could allow the United States to achieve *space control*. Terrestrial-based weapons and concepts for accomplishing both defensive counterspace and offensive counterspace will be compared to the space-based alternatives. Chapter 4 will focus on terrestrial alternatives to space-based *force application* weapons, including ballistic missile defense (BMD). Since many of the weapons discussed in these chapters are in the earliest phases of development, very little data regarding the expected cost of complete systems is available. Cost data is mentioned where it is available, but for the most part cost is treated qualitatively.

Chapter 5 provides a brief overview of the potential political implications of deciding to weaponize space. This topic is quite extensive and worthy of an extensive research effort in itself. Since others have already published works on this subject, this paper will only highlight the most significant implications, leaving further study to the interested reader.[10] Finally, Chapter 6 summarizes the conclusions that can be drawn from the material presented in this paper and offers recommendations about the next steps to be taken regarding the decision to weaponize space.

---

[10] To compliment Ziegler's paper cited above, a detailed look at the views of other members of the international community may be found in Pericles Gasparini Alves, *Prevention of an Arms Race in Outer Space: A Guide to the Discussions in the Conference on Disarmament*, UNIDIR/91/79, Annex A (United Nations, N.Y., United Nations Institute for Disarmament Research: 1991), Part II. For a discussion of the international political implications of space-based weapons for the United States, see Karl Mueller, "Space Weapons and U.S. Security: Why and How to Avert a Dangerous Potential Revolution," School of Advanced Airpower Studies, September 1997.

Chapter 2

Space-Based Weapons

What we want to do in or from space is affected greatly by our judgments as to what is technologically possible. Although we should not permit defense policy to be driven simply by what is technologically possible, regardless of careful consideration of strategic need and desirability, neither should we close our minds to the possibility that new technology may change dramatically the terms of strategic policy debate.

Colin S. Gray

American Military Space Policy

As Colin Gray aptly put it, the decision of whether or not to deploy weapons in space should not be based only on the fact that it is technologically possible to do so. It is equally important to determine if such weapons are truly needed. Creating new weapons merely because it is possible to do so can have unfortunate consequences. An historical example of such a technological imperative producing a weapon of questionable value is the Nazi rocket program of World War II. Approximately 2 billion marks (500 million 1942 dollars) produced enough V-2 rockets to deliver about 6000 tons of high explosives against the Allies—a quantity that is only about four times that dropped during a single RAF raid on the Peenemünde rocket development center itself.[11] While this effort was not the sole cause of the Nazi downfall, it certainly absorbed resources that could have

9

been better used elsewhere. The current era of austere defense budgets makes it imperative that the U.S. military avoid a similar miscalculation.

Because letting technology alone drive the development of weapons can have serious repercussions, it is necessary to evaluate weapon concepts carefully to determine whether or not they have the potential to serve national defense needs. The purpose of this chapter is to lay out the types of space-based weapons currently being considered for development, how they are envisioned to be used, and what *technological* factors bear on the decision to deploy them.

Missions for Space-Based Weapons

Space-based weapons are being considered for two categories of missions: space control and force application. The space control mission includes protecting U.S. and allied space assets, attacking enemy assets, and denying an enemy access to space. The primary means for accomplishing these tasks are either launch suppression, or destroying or degrading the performance of enemy satellites. These actions can be either defensive, protecting friendly assets, or offensive, denying the enemy the benefits of space-based assets. Potential force application missions include ballistic missile defense (BMD) and attacking airborne or terrestrial targets. Of these, BMD has received the most attention, even more than space control. The main reasons for this are the United States' pursuit of a high profile and costly BMD development program called the strategic defense

---

[11] Michael J. Neufeld, *The Rocket and the Reich*, Peenemünde and the Coming of the Ballistic Missile Era, (New York: The Free Press, 1995), 199, 282, 273.

initiative (SDI) (often referred to as Star Wars),[12] and the prohibition of space-based BMD systems in the 1972 ABM Treaty.

The concepts being explored to perform these tasks run the gamut from direct impact kinetic energy weapons to high-energy lasers that can destroy satellites across thousands of kilometers. The weapon concepts being explored for space control missions are very similar to those for force application missions; particularly those developed for BMD. In fact, many of the proposed weapons can be used for more than one mission. Because of this inherent multi-use nature, weapon concepts will be discussed individually, and prospective missions will be delineated for each of them.

Directed Energy Weapons (DEW)

Directed energy weapons include laser, radio frequency (RF), and particle beam weapons. Only the first two types of weapons will be discussed here since particle beam weapons have fallen out of favor for a variety of reasons.[13] Even lasers are not without their problems, and while the idea of reaching across thousands of kilometers at the speed of light to destroy a target is alluring,[14] the technical problems associated with this are considerable.

---

[12] In May 1993, the SDI was renamed the Ballistic Missile Defense Organization (BMDO) and was refocused to concentrate on ground-based defenses, primarily against theater missiles with a much smaller continuing effort aimed at a national missile defense capability. [Phillip Clark, ed., *Jane's Space Directory*, (Coulsdon, England: Jane's Information Group Ltd., Sentinel House, 1997), 165.

[13] Despite some promising results in a 1989 test, the U.S. neutral particle beam program was eventually cancelled in 1994. Aside from cost considerations, major remaining challenges included development of a suitable power source. [Clark, 169.]

[14] According to Dan Wildt, TRW's space-based laser integration program manager a space-based chemical laser "would have a 'lethal range' of 4,000 to 5,000 kilometers." [Joseph C. Anselmo, "New Funding Spurs Space Laser Efforts," *Aviation Week & Space Technology*, 14 October 1996, 67.]

Lasers

The potential for using lasers as weapons was recognized almost from the moment they were first discovered in 1960, but producing beams with enough power has always been problematic. Lasers have several characteristics that seem to make them ideal candidates for space-based weapons. Using lasers in space eliminates the need for them to compensate for distortion caused by atmospheric turbulence, a major concern for terrestrial laser weapon concepts.[15] A laser can strike at the speed of light and hit a target almost instantaneously. Since light has no mass, lasers are not constrained by orbital dynamics and can fire against any target within their line-of-sight. Unfortunately, lasers also have drawbacks that make using them as weapons more complicated than is often assumed.

The basic parts of a laser weapon system are the laser itself, its power supply, the systems necessary to track targets and point the laser, and the command and control systems necessary to employ it. Major sub-components of the laser itself are the lasing and resonance chamber, and the mirrors needed to focus and aim the beam. The size of these components, as well as that of the power source, vary with the type of laser and the beam power to be produced.

Laser beams can be created in a number of ways, and the characteristics of the beam depend on the manner of its creation. The first lasers used solid crystals such as rubies and have demonstrated the highest power levels, up to 10,000 megawatts, but only in very short pulses. Attempts to deliver more energy to a target by generating multiple pulses inevitably create heat build-up problems that shatter the crystals.[16] These lasers are also not very good at converting electricity into laser energy, with efficiencies generally less about 1-2 percent.[17] Continuous wave lasers, which emit a constant beam rather than pulses, have also been investigated and show greater promise for use as

---

[15] Turbulence distorts the wavefront of a laser beam as it travels through the atmosphere, lessening its ability to deliver energy to a target. The problem is greatly reduced when propagating a beam from space to the ground.
[16] Michael J. Muolo, *Space Handbook: An Analyst's Guide, Volume Two*, (Maxwell AFB, Ala.: Air University Press, December 1993), 251-2.
[17] Anthony E. Siegman, *Lasers*, (Mill Valley, CA: University Science Books), 68.

weapons. Each type of laser has its own drawbacks; the ones being considered for use as weapons attempt to mitigate these problems to arrive at a practical system.

The main problem with making a laser into a weapon is generating a reliable, high-power beam with good beam quality. For the role most often discussed, space-based BMD, the energy density necessary to fatally weaken the skin of a liquid-fueled ballistic missile may be as low as 1 KJ/cm^2.[18] The more robust construction of solid fuel ballistic missiles, coupled with fairly simple countermeasures (such as ablative coatings), may raise this level as high as 30 KJ/cm^2.[19] Richard Garwin, a physicist at IBM's Watson Lab and consultant for Los Alamos Science Lab, calculates that for a missile hardness of 20 KJ/cm^2, a laser must focus a 25 megawatt beam into a spot 1 meter in area for 6.7 seconds if it is to deliver energy to the target fast enough to burn through the casing.[20] This assumes the missile does not rotate, another relatively simple countermeasure. It is reasonable to assume that the testing and deployment of space-based laser weapons by the United States will prompt potential adversaries to take these basic precautions. For this

---

[18] Colin S. Gray, *American Military Space Policy: Information Systems, Weapon Systems and Arms Control*, (Cambridge, MA: Abt Books, 1982), 56.

[19] In contrast to a liquid fueled missile's thin aluminum skin containing highly volatile, pressurized fuel, a solid rocket motor uses a glass-reinforced plastic case coated with epoxy resin built to act as the combustion chamber. The considerably thicker walls of this design will require the laser to deliver more energy before it bursts. Examples of missiles that use this type of construction include most submarine launched ballistic missiles, the U.S. Minuteman III, the Peacekeeper, and the Army tactical missile system (ATACMS). [Colin S. Gray, *American Military Space Policy: Information Systems, Weapon Systems and Arms Control*, (Cambridge, MA: Abt Books, 1982), 56; Duncan Lennox, ed., *Jane's Strategic Weapon Systems*, (Coulsdon, England: Jane's Information Group Limited, Sentinel House, 1997), Tab: Offensive Weapons, Issue 26 January 1998.]

[20] Richard Garwin, "How Many Orbiting Lasers for Boost-Phase Intercept?" Nature, 315 (May 23, 1985), 286-90. Garwin also co-chaired a study by the Union of Concerned Scientists which discusses the feasibility of orbital lasers in detail. [John Tirman, ed., *The Fallacy of Star Wars*, (New York: Vintage Books, 1983),105.]

reason a laser capable of producing a 25 MW beam and focusing it into a spot of 1 m^2 at a range of 3,000 km for 7 seconds will form the baseline for discussion in this paper.[21]

To date, the most powerful continuous wave lasers created by the United States generate only 1-2 megawatts. While one current design (the Alpha laser) is said to be scalable to greater power levels, these higher power levels would require massive space structures. The lasing chamber of the Alpha laser (the chamber that produces the beam) is over 2 meters long and produces a "megawatt power" beam.[22] If this is interpreted to be 1-2 megawatts, and the optimistic assumption is made that the laser is linearly scalable, then the chamber would have to be 25-50 meters (82-164 ft) long in order to produce a 25 MW beam.[23]

Building lasers with enough power is only one of the hurdles to overcome before practical laser weapons become a reality. Other obstacles include creating highly reflective mirrors able to focus and direct the powerful beams without overheating. To point the mirrors, steerable assemblies precise and agile enough to maintain the beam on a moving target for the required seven seconds (for BMD) and then rapidly slew to another target must also be developed. The problem is that there is a relationship between the wavelength of the laser, mirror size, engagement range and power delivered to the target.[24] For ranges of 3,000 to 4,000 km, the laser's mirror would have to be 10 to

---

[21] The requirement of a 3,000 km range for a space-based laser is derived from analyses of the number of satellites required to provide global protection against a massive missile attack by the Soviet Union. [Richard Garwin, "How Many Orbiting Lasers for Boost-Phase Intercept?" *Nature*, 315 (23 May 1985), 288.] While current initiatives for orbital lasers are not intended to counter such a massive attack, this criterion still seems to be the baseline. Evidence of this is the development of components for an 11 m diameter light-weight mirror for the U.S. space-based laser program which implies a range of about 3,200 km. [J. London and H. Pike, "Fire In the Sky: U.S. Space Laser Development From 1968," (paper no. IAA-97-IAA.2.3.06), (American Institute of Aeronautics and Astronautics), 8.] Details on the relationship between range and mirror diameter are discussed in subsequent footnotes.

[22] The actual power levels achieved by military lasers are classified. For the purposes of this paper "megawatt power" is interpreted to be 1-2 megawatts. This is based on the assumption that power levels much above these would be referred to as "multi-megawatt." The term "megawatt power" was used in J. London and H. Pike, 6.

[23] The chamber probably cannot be made with a larger diameter because the flow of gasses through the chamber would be changed significantly. Similarly, flow rates for the chemicals probably cannot be increased since they are presumably optimized for maximum power already. This leaves lengthening the chamber as the only method for creating more powerful beams.

[24] Garwin, 288.

14 meters (33 – 45 ft) in diameter.[25] These mirrors must be pointed accurately enough to prevent deviations of more than tens of centimeters while the weapon travels about 50 km in one direction and the target travels about 40 km in another.[26] While aiming devices with the requisite precision and accuracy have been demonstrated,[27] these demonstrations have been made with the laser and its associated pointing equipment firmly bolted to the earth, not floating in space. The tests also did not have to track targets moving as fast as an ICBM, and have not incorporated the large mirrors necessary to handle lasers powerful enough to be weapons.

In order for a laser weapon's mirror to minimize phase error, it is created out of segments that are individually moved by actuators.[28] The large structures needed to support these mirrors are not quickly maneuvered for re-targeting. Although the BMDO estimates retargeting to require as little as "0.5 seconds for new targets requiring small

---

[25] These mirrors are for infrared lasers operating at a wavelength of 2.7 μm. The wavelength of the laser determines the beam diffraction, this in turn drives mirror size since the proper mirror size will minimize diffraction for a laser operating at a particular range. This relationship between wavelength, mirror diameter, and range, means that lasers using shorter wavelengths would require smaller mirrors. [$R=(\pi d/4\lambda)S$, where R is the range, d is the mirror diameter, λ is the wavelength of the laser, and S is the diameter of the spot the laser makes on the target] This paper assumes that laser weapons will have a perfect mirror of the optimum size for the weapon's range. [Hans Bethe and Richard Garwin, "Appendix A: New BMD Technologies," *Daedalus: Weapons in Space* II, no. 114 (Summer 1985), 338-9.]

[26] At an altitude of 1,300 km, the planned altitude for the U.S. space based laser, the weapon will be traveling at about 7.2 km/s and cover about 50 km during a seven second firing. [$v=sqrt(\mu/r)$, where r is the radius of the circular orbit and μ is the gravitational parameter for the earth (398,600 km^3/s^2)] The accelerating missile will cover a slightly shorter distance. [Dave Dooling, "Ballistic Missile Defense," *IEEE Spectrum*, September 1997, 59.] [Garwin, 288.]

[27] "In 1991, the space-borne Relay Mirror Experiment (RME), relayed low-power laser beam from a ground site to low-earth orbit and back down to a scoring target board with greater pointing accuracy than needed by SBL." [John Pike, "Space Based Laser," FAS Space Policy Project Special Weapons Monitor, 3, on-line, Internet, 7 February 1998, available from http://www.fas.org/spp/starwars/program/SBL.htm]

[28] When a laser beam is created it is composed of a single phase front and maintaining this front is essential to achieving maximum power. If the beam is to be effective at distances on the order of thousands of kilometers, it must be expanded to illuminate a large mirror that is designed to focus the beam so that it achieves its smallest spot size at the desired distance. Since fabricating a large single-piece mirror is extremely difficult (and almost as difficult to launch), large mirrors are created from smaller segments that can be individually adjusted. Doing this makes it possible to minimize distortions so that the beam leaving the focusing mirror maintains its single phase front.

angle changes,"[29] this seems optimistic. A point of reference that runs counter to this claim is the Hubble space telescope, which has a three second settling time for even the smallest adjustments and takes several minutes for re-targeting. While it is not designed to be a weapon, the Hubble space telescope is much smaller, with a single-piece mirror that is only 2.4 meters in diameter.[30] The momentum that must be overcome to maneuver larger structures will likely require similar amounts of time even if significant advances are made. While BMD lasers may not need to be moved through large angles for re-aiming if the targets are clustered together, more dispersed targets may require this capability.

The type of laser currently being developed for use as a weapon is the chemical laser. This variety produces a beam by mixing chemicals at low pressure. When mixed, these chemicals react in a way very similar to rocket fuel, but in this case the result is intense light with the energy concentrated in a very narrow band of wavelengths. The products of the combustion are high-temperature corrosive gases that must be continuously removed from the chamber for the lasing process to continue. One of the major problems to be overcome if lasers are to be successfully made into space-based weapons is providing enough chemical fuel to power them. The lasers will consume approximately 375 - 750 kilograms of chemicals per second, and engaging 10 ballistic missiles requiring 7 seconds each would require 26,250 – 52,500 kg (57,750-115,500 lbs) of chemicals.[31] Supplying these chemicals to an orbiting satellite would be a major logistical challenge. The need for large quantities of chemicals appears to make space-based chemical lasers unfeasible, but with efficiencies of about 25 percent, chemical

[29] Ballistic Missile Defense Organization Fact Sheet 97-09, Ballistic Missile Defense Organization, The Pentagon, Washington D.C., 2.
[30] Bethe and Garwin, 339.
[31] The Star Lite demonstration laser satellite will require 30 kg/s to "operate at megawatt levels" according to LTC John London, the Space-Based Laser program integrator at the Ballistic Missile Defense Organization. [Interviewed by Dave Dooling, "Ballistic Missile Defense," *IEEE Spectrum*, September 1997, 59.] With the assumption that "megawatt levels" means 1–2 megawatts, 25 megawatts should require a reactant flow 12.5 to 25 times greater (375 – 750 kg/s) assuming linear scalability. This latter assumption may be somewhat optimistic considering the dynamics of chemical lasers.

lasers have the best combination of efficiency and power generation of any lasers being investigated today.[32]

The mechanics of processing large quantities of gas to generate the laser beam also complicate the system. Current plans call for venting the spent gas overboard in order to dispose of it.[33] It is assumed that the vacuum of space will prevent the hot corrosive gasses from damaging the laser, however with flow rates of hundreds of kilograms per second there may be a tendency for the gas to form a cloud around the satellite. It will also be necessary to vent the exhaust in multiple directions so that the resulting forces cancel each other out and do not move the satellite.

Chemical lasers appear to have serious drawbacks, but the alternatives are even less promising. Lasers that require electricity to generate the beam have been largely eliminated from consideration as weapons because of the difficulty in generating enough power in space. Compared to chemical laser efficiencies of 25 percent, the 0.01 percent efficiency of electrically driven helium-neon lasers is paltry indeed.[34] Due to the inherent losses in generating electricity in the first place, the conversion efficiency of an electrically driven laser makes finding an adequate power source a major problem.

Even if electrically driven lasers were 100 percent efficient at converting electricity into beam power, this approach would be impractical. Unless nuclear power is used, it is probably not even *possible* to generate enough electrical power.[35] Solar power is impractical because at 130 w/ft^2, solar energy is not dense enough to power a weapon.[36] Even if 100 percent of the solar energy available were converted into laser energy, it

---

[32] Geoffrey E. Forden, "COILed to Strike," *IEEE Spectrum*, September 1997, 46.

[33] Dooling, "Ballistic Missile Defense," 58.

[34] Siegman, 65.

[35] Even using nuclear power would be problematic. The reactors required to produce the 25 megawatts needed for a laser, assuming 100% conversion from electrical to laser energy, are not the type currently used in space. For instance, the controversial Cassini space probe, launched in October 1997, used a plutonium-based reactor that only produced an average power of 745 watts. [Karl Grossman, "Nuclear Gamble," *The Progressive*, September 1997, 20.] Even the Topaz 2 reactor purchased from Russia by the Bush Administration is only thought to be scalable up to 50-70 kW, not the megawatt levels needed for laser weapons. ["Topaz 2 Go-Ahead to Speed U.S. Thermionic Effort," *Aviation Week & Space Technology*, 6 April 1992, 28.] Reactors capable of producing enough power for lasers would need to be of an entirely new kind. Such a reactor would entail a development program of its own, provided a design with enough capacity is even feasible.

would take about 192,000 square feet of solar collectors to produce the 25 megawatts necessary for a laser weapon. Given the limitations of today's technology, solar cells only produce about 10 watts per pound. This means that a 25 megawatt laser would require 2.5 million pounds of solar cells, and this figure does not include the batteries that would be needed to store the energy if the weapon was to be useable in the absence of sunlight. Even if current efforts to increase solar cell efficiency to 50 watts per pound are successful, 500,000 lbs just for solar cells is still impractical. It becomes apparent that despite their drawbacks, chemical lasers are the best such option available today.

Another constraint is imposed by the need to keep ranges down to 3000 to 4000 km, at least for engaging ballistic missiles. To do this, the lasers must be in fairly low orbits of about 1000 km. Low orbits in turn require a large number of satellites if continuous coverage of a target area is to be maintained. For example, in the BMD role the number of satellites required to stop a massive missile launch (1400 missiles) from the Soviet Union would have been 460 even under very optimistic assumptions.[37] Obviously if the projected threat comprises significantly fewer missiles, then the number of satellites can be reduced.

The current U.S. program to develop laser weapons for the BMD mission is the space-based laser program (SBL). The objective of this program is to provide the United States with a BMD system effective against both short-range (theater) and intercontinental ballistic missiles. To defend against ballistic missiles, the SBL would engage them in the boost phase while they were still accelerating. Destroying a missile early is important because once the rocket motor cuts off it has enough velocity to reach the target country. Boost-phase destruction causes the missile to fall short of the target, ideally on the enemy's territory. The front-running candidate for the SBL is a hydrogen-fluoride chemical laser based on the Alpha laser developed under the Strategic Defense Initiative. In 1991 this laser demonstrated the capability to produce "megawatt power" in a simulated space environment. According to Lieutenant Colonel John London, the

---

[36] Muolo, *Space Handbook Vol. Two*, 151.

[37] Optimistic assumptions include instantaneous re-targeting and only 5 seconds needed to destroy a missile. Further derivations raise the number to 1344 satellites to stop a 3,000 missile launch, assuming perfect reliability. Detailed calculations arriving at these numbers may be found in Bethe and Garwin, 339-43.

Space-Based Laser program integrator at the Ballistic Missile Defense Organization, the envisioned system would consist of a constellation of 20 satellites operating at an altitude of 1300 km and would provide "planetary coverage" for both theater and intercontinental ballistic missiles.[38] Using consumption rates of 375-750 kg/s, this system would require 1,155,000 to 2,310,000 pounds of chemicals just to give each of 20 weapons the ability to fire 10 bursts of 7 seconds each. This is more than just a small logistical problem; it is a fundamental weakness of the concept.[39]

The space control mission also appears to be an ideal one for orbital lasers. The great distances inherent in space operations, coupled with the large amounts of energy required to change orbits, poses considerable problems when attempting to physically intercept an enemy satellite. Using lasers as antisatellite (ASAT) weapons seems to offer the prospect of sidestepping these problems in the same way that they do for ballistic missile defense. Unfortunately, designing orbital lasers to attack satellites incurs many of the same problems encountered with designing them to attack ballistic missiles, although the physical characteristics of satellites may make them easier to damage.

If they could be built, orbital lasers with the ability to destroy ballistic missiles in the boost phase would probably also be capable of destroying satellites. Orbital dynamics ensures that the relative velocity between two satellites in similar orbits would probably be within the range of velocities for which an orbital laser designed to engage an ascending ballistic missile would have to contend. The pointing accuracy and tracking capability needed for a BMD laser should also be adequate to track a satellite in a crossing orbit, a situation where the need to quickly slew the weapon would be the

---

[38] Dooling, "Ballistic Missile Defense," 59; and Ballistic Missile Defense Organization Fact Sheet 97-09, Ballistic Missile Defense Organization, The Pentagon, Washington D.C., 2.
[39] The total number of missiles the system would be able to destroy is not given in Dooling, London and Pike, or BMDO fact sheet 97-09.

greatest.[40] Similarly, the range at which BMD lasers are being designed to operate would also be adequate for the ASAT mission. However, designing an orbital laser to be effective against both ballistic missiles and satellites would require some additional capability.

Satellites have some characteristics that make using lasers against them difficult. The "kill mechanism" by which lasers can destroy satellites is different from that used to destroy ballistic missiles. Ballistic missiles have an extremely bright infrared signature during launch and a fragile structure that would collapse catastrophically, and visibly, if significantly damaged. Satellites are built quite differently. While satellites generally have delicate components, such as solar cells and optical sensors, that are vulnerable to laser attack, the destruction of these components would be difficult to verify. Causing greater damage, or damaging satellites without vulnerable sensors, may be necessary for verification purposes. Determining which part of a satellite to target, and then focusing the beam on that part for the requisite length of time, promises to be no more difficult than focusing a laser on an ascending ballistic missile. However, the much fainter infrared signatures of satellites also require a different mechanism for target acquisition and tracking.

An additional point to consider when deciding whether or not to use orbital lasers in the ASAT role, is that it would probably be necessary to place them in orbits different from those optimized for BMD. Ideally an ASAT laser would be placed in an orbit that allowed it to pass within lethal range of the maximum number of targets, albeit over a considerable period of time. Such an orbit is unlikely to be the same as those of a satellite constellation optimized to keep the most likely missile threats within range. This fact would diminish any savings to be gained by exploiting the multi-use nature of orbital lasers.

---

[40] An orbital laser designed for BMD would have to be able to engage a missile launched on an intersecting trajectory that crossed at 90 degrees to the laser. The crossing velocity during such an engagement would be close to the burn-out velocity of the ballistic missile, about 5 km/s. If such a weapon was to be capable of engaging a missile at fairly close range, then it must be capable of moving at a fairly high angular rate. In contrast, a low earth satellite crossing the laser's orbit at 90 degrees would cross at a higher velocity (about 7 km/s), but could be engaged at a range that would keep the needed angular rate within the capability of the weapon.

One problem orbital lasers definitely will not be able to solve is the difficulty associated with attacking satellites at truly long distances. Ideally, an ASAT laser would be able to attack more than just the satellites in neighboring orbits. Unfortunately, the problems of constructing a laser capable of engaging targets at a range of 3,000 km are compounded as the range increases. For instance, if a weapon in low earth orbit (LEO)[41] were to engage military communication satellites in geosynchronous orbits, it would need a range of almost 30,000 km.[42] Designing a weapon with such a long range increases the size of the mirror needed to focus the beam, unless shorter wavelength lasers can be devised. As mentioned above, there is a direct relationship between mirror size and the range of the weapon. A laser that had a range of 30,000 km would require a mirror 99 meters (325 ft) in diameter if current chemical lasers were to be used. These large mirrors must also be agile enough to keep the laser beam on the target long enough to do damage. Building such enormous structures capable of maneuvering with this much agility would be a major technological achievement.

To overcome the difficulty of operating at extremely long range, it would be possible to deploy some weapons in orbits just below GEO, for instance 3,000 km lower so that the lasers being developed for BMD could be used. Unfortunately the cost of doing so would be very high. If the massive weapons envisioned for BMD were to be placed in orbits with an altitude of 27,000 km, which would allow them to cruise past a satellite in GEO about every 16½ hours, then massive boosters would be required, both to deploy them initially and to refuel the lasers if it became necessary. While lasers

---

[41] Low earth orbits are considered to be those with altitudes up to 2,000 km. [John V. Evans, "New Satellites for Personal Communications," *Scientific American*, April 1998, 73.]

[42] Assuming the most favorable alignment of a LEO weapon in a 1000 km orbit, firing from directly beneath the higher altitude satellite, the laser would need a range of about 29,000 km to reach a satellite in GEO. (GEO satellites orbit at an altitude of about 30,000 km.)

operating at shorter wavelengths would solve some of these problems,[43] these lasers have yet to produce enough power to be feasible weapons.[44]

Thus if a space-based laser could be made to work as a BMD weapon, it could also be modified to have considerable ASAT capability. The primary changes needed for this new mission would be the ability to detect the much fainter infrared signature of distant satellites, and to deploy the weapons in orbits optimized for antisatellite operations. While some target satellites would pass within lethal range of SBL platforms dedicated to BMD, using precious shots from the only weapon capable of intercepting a ballistic missile in the boost phase, just to destroy a satellite, may not be wise. Conversely, dedicating weapons as sophisticated as orbital lasers to antisatellite operations, by deploying them into ASAT-optimized orbits, would be an expensive solution. These considerations become particularly germane when orbital lasers are compared with the other options for performing the space control mission that will be discussed in Chapter 3.

Another proposed use for space-based lasers is the force application mission of attacking airborne or surface targets. However, the only laser being considered for development as an orbital weapon is the Alpha chemical laser that operates at a wavelength of 2.7 microns.[45] This wavelength was chosen in part because the laser energy is heavily absorbed by water vapor in the atmosphere, which is considered to be a safety feature because it prevents unintended collateral damage when ballistic missiles are

---

[43] For example a laser operating at ultraviolet wavelengths could be focused into a 1 meter diameter spot at a range of 30,000 km using a mirror only about 11 meters in diameter. Unfortunately the infrared telescope needed to track a ballistic missile, or satellite, at these ranges would still need a mirror 100 to 150 meters in diameter. Visible light telescopes would be smaller, but they offer the opponent more options for countermeasures, such as painting the satellite black. Infrared signatures, on the other hand, are virtually impossible to suppress in space. (It should be noted that black satellites would have severe heat build-up problems that would make their infrared signature even more pronounced.) [John Tirman, ed., *The Fallacy of Star Wars*, (New York, NY: Vintage Books, 1983),105.]

[44] Geoffrey E. Forden, "A Panoply of Lasers," *IEEE Spectrum*, September 1997, 42.

[45] London and Pike, 3.

being engaged.[46] While this may be a safety feature for the SBL, it makes the laser of little use for engaging airborne or surface targets.

Using other wavelengths could allow space-based lasers to have some capability against airborne and surface targets. If shorter wavelengths were used, another advantage would be that the mirrors that aim the beams could be made smaller.[47] Unfortunately, there remains the major problem of producing a laser with a significantly better combination of wavelength and power.

While Alpha-type lasers would be ineffective against surface targets, the nature of airborne targets makes any such weapons of questionable use even against high-flying aircraft. While combat aircraft are specifically designed to be able to withstand considerable damage and still complete their mission, the cockpit canopy of an aircraft is vulnerable to laser attack. In fact, the types of lasers being considered for BMD weapons are very effective at vaporizing Plexiglas, provided they can dwell on the target for long enough. Something that may make this difficult is that the flight path of an aircraft is much less predictable than that of a missile, although this may be offset by the fact that they also move much more slowly. However, given the power levels required of BMD lasers, it is probable that burning through the canopy of an aircraft at high altitude would not be difficult.

Provided a space-based laser were powerful enough to penetrate the canopy of an aircraft, there is still the problem that the detection and tracking system needed for attacking aircraft would be very different from one which exploits the very hot and bright plume of a ballistic missile, or the reflected light of a satellite against the background of space. This is because it would be very difficult to use an optical or infrared tracking system to detect and track the relatively small, cool signature of an aircraft against the background of the earth. Furthermore, the weapon would need some means of determining where on the aircraft the beam must be focused, a far from trivial problem at the ranges involved. Giving an orbital laser the ability to detect and track aircraft would

---

[46] According to TRW's space-based laser integration program manager, Dan Wildt, "the beam would be absorbed by water vapor before it reached the surface of the Earth." [Anselmo, "New Funding Spurs Space Laser Efforts," 67.]

[47] For instance, an ultraviolet laser (operating at 0.3μ) with the same range as the SBL would need a mirror only 3.75 meters in diameter.

require yet another set of sensors and additional software to overcome these problems. Changes such as these would add cost and complexity to an already expensive weapon.

Similar to giving BMD lasers an ASAT capability, the addition of a counterair capability would further complicate the decision of which targets to attack. Fuel limitations would mean that every aircraft engaged would be one less ballistic missile (or satellite) that could be shot down. Given the fact that there are other weapons that are very good at shooting down aircraft, and that the same is not true of ballistic missiles, using lasers to engage high-flying aircraft does not appear very attractive.

Another a potential obstacle to using space-based lasers against airborne targets may be the 1980 United Nations Conventional Weapons Convention. This convention, or more specifically Protocol IV, signed in January 1997, prohibits using weapons that are designed "as one of their combat functions to cause permanent blindness to unenhanced vision."[48] As long as a space-based laser is designed to destroy the aircraft or kill the pilot, it would be legal. But if the laser lacks the power to do more than blind the pilot, then using it against aircraft could be deemed illegal. This situation may not be as farfetched as it initially appears. If an orbital laser were designed primarily for other missions, its capability against aircraft could very easily be limited to blinding the pilot. Using it in such a mode would clearly be illegal, and citing this potential capability as part of a rationale for developing the system would only bolster the arguments of those who oppose it.[49]

Once the problems of transforming a laser into a viable weapon have been solved, it will still be necessary to make it robust enough to survive years of inactivity in the hostile environment of space. From the threat of being struck by space debris, to

---

[48] W. Hays Parks, "Memorandum of Law: Trauvaux Preparatoires and Legal Analysis of Blinding Laser Weapons Protocol," *The Army Lawyer*, June 1997, DA-PAM 27-50-295), 33-41. The protocol went into force on 30 January 1998 when it was ratified by the 20th nation, Hungary. [Thalif Deen, "UN protocol brings laser blinding ban into force," *Jane's Defense Weekly*, 11 February 1998, 6.]

[49] It should be noted that the Alpha laser is considered to be "eye-safe" since it operates at a wavelength greater then 1.44 µm, although at the power levels under discussion here it would probably boil the water in a pilot's eyes if the explosive decompression of burning through the cockpit canopy wasn't enough to throw the aircraft out of control and break the laser weapon's "lock." Were they to be used in order to reduce mirror size and improve atmospheric penetration, wavelengths shorter than 1.44 microns could be limited to blinding pilots if they were used at their maximum range.

environmental factors such as radiation, charged particle bombardment, and the thermal cycling inherent in the frequent passages from day to night, space is a challenging environment in which to operate. While all satellites must contend with these problems, lasers are particularly delicate. Lasers are extremely dependent on the precise alignment of their components if they are to work. As demonstrated by the near failure of a recent test of the MIRACL laser, it is difficult to get a high-power laser to work reliably on the ground.[50] Building such a laser to withstand the rigors of launch and subsequent storage in orbit will be extremely challenging. Couple these difficulties with the consequences of failure, since weapons by definition are only used in times of dire need, and the prospects of a feasible space-based laser grow much dimmer.

To be practical as space-based weapons, lasers must be devised that combine the qualities of high efficiency, short wavelength, high power, and low cost in a package robust enough to withstand the rigors of space. With all of these hurdles to overcome, a space-based laser weapon will not be feasible without a number of fundamental breakthroughs in laser physics and engineering.

Radio Frequency (RF) Weapons

Another family of directed energy weapons are radio frequency (RF) weapons. These weapons would be deployed in geosynchronous orbit and use large antennas to direct RF energy at enemy electronic systems. RF weapons would use very large antennas the size of which would determine the size of the beam reaching the Earth's surface. Antennae diameters of 100 meters would yield 6 mile diameter beams while 1000 meter diameter antennas could produce much more intense beams as small as 1 mile in diameter. Within the beam's footprint, power densities would be about 10 w/m^2 and could burn out unprotected electronics and thoroughly disrupt even shielded systems.[51]

---

[50] Bill Gertz, "Shared satellite laser test weighed," *The Washington Times*, 2 January 1998, A1.
[51] *New World Vistas, Air and Space Power for the 21st Century, Space Applications Volume* (Washington D.C.: USAF Scientific Advisory Board, 1995), 84-5.

A major factor weighing against RF weapons is the considerable technological advances necessary to make them feasible.[52] One major obstacle is the development of the advanced antennas that would be necessary. While it may eventually be possible to construct inflatable structures for antennas that are 100 meters in diameter,[53] larger antennas are envisioned to use a "virtual" structure where hundreds or thousands of micro-satellites would be arranged in a very precise formation and operate in concert. The difficulty lies in the fact that each of them must maintain position relative to the others. Constantly changing position precisely enough to create a "virtual" structure will require large amounts of maneuvering propellant and is unlikely to be feasible within the foreseeable future.[54]

Considering the hurdles in orbital antenna technology that must be overcome before space-based directed-energy weapons are feasible, it is unlikely that such systems can be fielded until the cost of routine access to space is reduced to the point that extensive experimentation can be undertaken. In light of this, technologically less challenging weapons are also being investigated.

---

[52] Surprisingly, generating enough power is not a problem for RF weapons. Between the much lower power densities necessary to damage electronics with electromagnetic radiation, and the huge "gain" achieved by advanced antenna designs (the projected 130 dB gain of a 100 meter diameter antenna would produce a 10 million megawatt beam from a 100 kW power source) the power requirements are quite modest, especially when compared to lasers. [*New World Vistas, Air and Space Power for the 21st Century, Space Applications Volume*, 84-5]

[53] Space Shuttle mission 77, launched on 19 May 1996, carried "the most complex and precise inflatable space structure ever," an inflatable antenna measuring about 15 m (50 ft) in diameter. [Michael A. Dornheim and Joseph C. Anselmo, "Complex Antenna Is Star of Mission 77," *Aviation Week & Space Technology*, 27 May 1996, 58-9.] The experiment was perhaps the first step toward the RF weapons described in New World Vistas. While the experiment did not actually test the transmission or reception capabilities of the antenna, the inflation and control tests were considered to be successful. Many more tests will be necessary before antennas as large as 100 meters in diameter will be feasible.

[54] Since each satellite would be in its own orbit around the earth, those that are not either in front of or following the center satellite would be in different orbital planes. Since they are in their own orbits, the satellites on either side of the center satellite would change sides twice during each orbit, crossing the center each time they crossed the equator. While it may be theoretically possible to maintain position relative to the center of the formation, each satellite would require a large amount of propellant to do so. For an overview of the orbital mechanics that lead to this conclusion see Muolo, *Space Handbook Vol. Two*, 23-81.

Direct Impact Weapons

Although laser and RF weapons appear to have many desirable properties, direct impact weapons are more feasible given current technology. Weapons that use either kinetic energy or that pass near enough to a target for an exploding fragmentation device to destroy it are being considered for a number of applications. In the arena of space control, antisatellite weapons using each of these methods have been proposed and tested. For the force application mission, space-based weapons using these methods have been proposed for attacking surface and airborne targets.

Kinetic Energy Antisatellite Weapons (KE ASATs)

Direct impact KE weapons rely on the large velocity differentials inherent in orbital dynamics to destroy a target. Given that a satellite in LEO travels at a velocity of approximately 7.8 kilometers per second (km/s), and that one pound of anything moving at 3 km/s has kinetic energy equivalent to a pound of high explosive,[55] hitting something at these speeds can be catastrophic. If the target is as fragile as a satellite, then only small amounts of mass are needed for destruction upon impact. However the problem of actually hitting a target is complex.

A space-based KE ASAT must be placed in an orbit that allows for a responsive intercept time. While there are a multitude of orbits that can accomplish this for any given target, the easiest way to visualize the problem is to consider an orbit that crosses the target's orbit numerous times during a day. If the ASAT's orbit is either higher or lower than that of the target, a relatively small booster motor could change it so that the ASAT intersects the target's orbit. Using the most economical transfer orbit would require only modest amounts of propellant, although it would be necessary to time the intercept so that the target would be at the intersection point of the orbits when the ASAT

---

[55] Joseph A. Smith, Advanced Concepts Engineer, Lawrence Livermore Laboratories, interviewed by the author, 11 February 1998.

arrived.[56] An important consideration for a space-based ASAT is preventing the enemy from knowing that a satellite is in fact a weapon. Fortunately non-ASAT satellites are placed in a wide variety of orbits and an ASAT could almost always be placed in a suitable orbit that would not reveal its nature.

A cursory overview of the interception process makes it seem fairly straightforward. For the United States, tracking satellites is not a difficult task, but in order to destroy one it is necessary to predict its future position with a high degree of accuracy. This accuracy is needed so that the interceptor can be placed close enough to the target for on-board sensors to see the target and make the final corrections needed for a direct impact. These last two steps are the most challenging.

What makes intercepting satellites so difficult is the combination of the large closing velocity inherent in KE space weapons and the relatively small size of the target. While the largest satellites may be about the size of a Greyhound bus, this bus is traveling at 7.8 km/s in LEO, about 17,500 miles per hour. In addition to the velocity of the target, the velocity of the intercepting weapon adds a complicating factor. Since the orbital altitude of a satellite determines its velocity, at the point of interception the velocities of the two satellites may be similar in magnitude, but different in direction.[57] Thus the closing velocity will be the vector sum of the velocities of the target and the weapon. Since KE ASATs rely on the velocity differential for destructive energy, it is necessary to keep closing velocities fairly high, a factor which complicates the interception process.

Once placed in an intersecting orbit, the interceptor must be able to "see" the target far enough away to allow it to make the final corrections needed for interception. This maneuver is not trivial even for the low closing velocities of 1,000 to 2,000 mph that are typical of air-to-air missiles fired at aircraft. Closing speeds more than 10 times greater make hitting a satellite much more difficult. Since only a direct impact will destroy the target, it is essential to determine the target's position and velocity with a

---

[56] With a little more fuel, a considerable number of trajectories that could decrease the time required to intercept would be possible, but in the majority of cases it would take more than one orbital period. For an in-depth tutorial on orbital trajectories, orbital maneuvers and orbital dynamics in general see Roger R. Bate, Donald D. Mueller, Jerry E. White, *Fundamentals of Astrodynamics*, (New York: Dover Publications Inc., 1971).

great degree of accuracy. The combination of needing to see a target at long range coupled with the agility necessary to make timely adjustments yields a complex weapon. While steps can be taken to increase the probability of a hit, such as dispersing a cloud of small steel pellets, the problem of ensuring a "kill" is still a difficult one. It should be noted that the feasibility of a KE weapon has already been demonstrated by the United States, while a co-orbital system was demonstrated by the Soviet Union, although both of these systems were ground based.[58]

Co-orbital ASAT

Another method for attacking enemy satellites is a co-orbital or near co-orbital approach. A co-orbital ASAT is one that closes slowly with its target, similar to the Space Shuttle rendezvousing with satellites in need of repair. A co-orbital ASAT uses an exploding warhead to destroy the target rather than the kinetic energy from a velocity differential. The main problem with this type of ASAT is that it usually takes at least one orbital period, about ninety minutes for LEO and longer for higher orbits, to match orbits with the target satellite. If the ASAT is to remain inconspicuous (i.e. if the ASAT's orbit is to disguise the nature of the weapon), this method will also require that it make larger maneuvers than a KE weapon if it is to complete an interception, especially if the target is in a different orbital plane. These factors dictate an interceptor with more maneuvering capability than an ASAT using a high-speed impact, although the interceptor would not have to be as agile.

Once a co-orbital vehicle starts on its intercept course, the target's owners could detect the maneuver and initiate countermeasures. The long time to interception may give the target time for either defensive actions or evasive maneuvers, depending on its capability. Between the slower intercept and the requirement for a larger more

---

[57] If the interceptor satellite is descending from a higher orbit, or ascending from a lower orbit, then its velocity will be higher or lower than that of the target respectively.
[58] "Defense Dept. Plans Next Test Firing of Air-Launched ASAT System," *Aviation Week & Space Technology*, 23 September 1985, 20. Richard L. Garwin, Kurt Gottfried and Donald L. Hafner, "Antisatellite Weapons," *Scientific American* 250, no. 6, June 1984, 47-9.

maneuverable vehicle, the high-speed (KE) approach seems to hold the most promise for a direct impact weapon.

Space Mines

An additional ASAT concept is the "space mine." This type of weapon is similar to the co-orbital ASAT just discussed, except in this case the weapon is placed into an orbit near the target satellite well before any hostilities break out. The problems inherent with this approach are similar to those of the co-orbital ASAT, compounded by the need to make the approach unobserved. As mentioned above, attempting to close with another satellite usually requires a large vehicle expending large quantities of propellant. In contrast, a viable space mine would require a more covert method of approach.

One method is to design a very small "stealth" weapon that is slowly moved into position over a long period of time. The weapon's orbit can be chosen so that it will not approach the target for days or weeks after launch, essential if an adversary isn't to become suspicious. When it does approach the target, the weapon will have a low relative velocity. If done properly, only a short firing of the thruster will then be required to match orbits and "park" the weapon near the target. When needed, the weapon can be activated and destroy the target by closing the final distance and exploding. The problem with this concept is that this type of weapon must be deployed well in advance of when it is needed, a fact that places considerable demands on its design.

One major problem with the space-mine is the need to perform station-keeping maneuvers (in order to keep itself near the target) while simultaneously keeping its most stealthy aspect pointed toward the earth (in order of avoid detection). Most potential target satellites maneuver often in order to accomplish their mission, and even targets in geostationary orbits must make adjustments to maintain their position. These maneuvers will have to be mimicked by the mine if it is to maintain its position relative to the target. Thus the mine should be small and stealthy to avoid detection, but may need a considerable amount of propellant to do its job. While there are electrically driven ion thrusters that do not consume much propellant, they require large amounts of power and produce only microscopic amounts of thrust.[59]

Another major problem associated with designing a long-lived space mine is providing a power source for the weapon. Since it may be many years before the mine is detonated, a long-term power source is necessary. If an electric propulsion system is used, this problem becomes even more critical. Most satellites meet their electrical needs by using solar power. However solar panels are not very compatible with a stealth satellite because they cannot always be oriented to provide a minimal radar cross-section. Most other power sources, such as batteries or fuel cells, cannot provide enough power for long enough to do the job. One potential solution, nuclear power, has other problems. Aside from the political outcry against using nuclear power in orbit, which may not matter with a weapon whose utility depends on absolute secrecy, the thermal signature of a nuclear powered satellite may make it less than ideal for a space mine.[60] While breakthroughs in technology may someday provide the means for surmounting the problems inherent in creating effective space mines, the costs of doing so may well be significant.[61]

KE Weapons for Force Application

Kinetic-energy weapons are also being considered for the force application missions of ballistic missile defense and orbital bombardment of very hard, high-value,

---

[59] For instance 200 kilowatts are required for a single motor to produce 1 lb of thrust. In light of the discussion made with respect to lasers, the size of a power source needed to provide 200 kW over long periods of time would probably forfeit most of the savings in size over conventional propulsion. In addition, such small thrust levels may be inadequate for keeping the space mine close to a maneuvering satellite. [Details about ion motor thrust levels and power requirements can be found in Muolo, *Space Handbook Vol. Two*, 130-32.]

[60] Ibid., 154-57.

[61] It would be much easier to develop a non-stealth space mine, since such a weapon would avoid the greatest obstacles associated with one which must remain undetected. However, the United States is unlikely to pursue such a weapon. Not only would its deployment mark a clear break from the traditional sanctuary status of space, it would yield few benefits in return. The low-tech nature of an overt space mine would make it relatively easy for other nations to duplicate, and given the fact that the United States has demonstrated the ability to destroy satellites with lower profile ground-based weapons (and that there are relatively few satellites we would want to destroy in the first place) it offers few benefits.

terrestrial targets. Orbital bombardment seeks to destroy targets by converting the kinetic energy associated with the weapon's high velocity (5 to 11 km/s) into work and heat. Such projectiles could have a number of configurations, including long thin rods, ultra-hard penetrating warheads, or warheads that fragment shortly before impact.

As with most weapons, trade-offs must be made when designing weapons for orbital bombardment. To attain velocities in the range of 10 to 11 km/s, satellites must be in orbits with an altitude of more than 40,000 km, but these high-altitude orbits sacrifice responsiveness to achieve high impact velocities. For instance, a weapon in a 40,000 km orbit would need about 5 hours to reach the earth's surface and would have an impact velocity of about 10 km/s. The actual time required to hit a specific target would probably be longer since it is unlikely that the weapon would be in the proper position to initiate an immediate attack. Lower orbits could yield shorter response times; for instance a satellite placed in a 500 mile (926 km) orbit could strike in less than 12 minutes if the orbital geometry was ideal. The trade-off is that a weapon in LEO would impact at less than 5 km/s.[62]

One design for such a KE projectile is a thin, heavy, metallic rod one to two meters in length. Such a weapon could be used against hard targets that are not too deeply buried. Depending on what they are made of, the rods can penetrate two to three times their length into a target. As long as the rod impacts at a velocity in excess of 3 km/s, the depth it penetrates depends exclusively on the composition of the target and the rod, with only slight differences among specific "hard" target materials.[63] The mechanism used for penetration is progressive erosion of the tip of the rod coupled with progressive erosion of the substance being penetrated. The pressure generated at the tip of rod causes both the rod and the target to liquefy in the vicinity of the tip. As the rod

---

[62] A satellite deorbited over the North Pole and impacting at 60 degrees north latitude would impact at approximately 5.1 km/s if it were assumed that the earth has no atmosphere. The atmospheric drag due to reentry would slow the weapon somewhat, but this can be minimized by proper design. Calculating the precise impact velocity of a theoretical weapon shape is beyond the scope of this paper.

penetrates the target, its progress is similar to that of a high-pressure jet of water penetrating earth. The results of hitting a target with one of these rods is similar to boring a hole, placing in the hole an amount of explosive comparable in weight to that of the rod, and detonating it. For example, a two-meter rod weighing 50 pounds and penetrating to a depth of 6 to 8 meters is similar to detonating 50 pounds of explosive in a hole slightly larger in diameter than the rod. As long as the rod penetrates to the interior of the target, the results are devastating.[64] A drawback of this type of weapon is that very deep targets would necessitate rods too massive to be practical.[65]

Another method for making use of the high velocities provided by orbital weapons is to use an ultra-hard penetrator with an explosive warhead. With this approach the weapon remains intact and can penetrate much deeper than eroding rods. After it has reached a preset depth, based on time from initial impact, or enters a zone of low resistance, like a room or tunnel, the warhead detonates. From a feasibility standpoint, materials hard enough to remain intact during the penetration phase are still being investigated. While these materials may make impact velocities of up to 4 km/s possible, this capability has yet to be demonstrated. Materials readily available, such as tungsten carbide, are generally unable to withstand impact at velocities much in excess of 1.5 km/s; above this velocity the weapon has the characteristics of a very short eroding rod.[66]

For orbital bombardment of softer targets, a weapon could be designed to slow down considerably before impact. Since speeds of Mach 6 to 8 (4,500 to 6,000 mph) are all that is necessary for small hardened projectiles to penetrate all but the most heavily

---

[63] Above 3 km/s, the depth of penetration is a function of the square root of the density ratio of the rod to the target material $[\sqrt{(\rho_{rod}/\rho_{target})}]$ and is largely unaffected by increasing the impact velocity. For example, a tungsten rod penetrating concrete will penetrate approximately three times its own length. Joseph A. Smith, Advanced Concepts Engineer, Lawrence Livermore Laboratories, interviewed by the author 12 May 1998.

[64] Ibid.

[65] A length-to-diameter ratio of 15 to 20 is required for these weapons to be effective. [Ibid.] As an example, a rod 3 meters long and 15 cm in diameter would have length-to-diameter ratio of 20. If this rod was made from tungsten (density 19.3 gm/cm^3), then it would weigh 1,022 kg (2,250 lbs). This is rather massive for a device to penetrate only about 9 meters (30 ft). In order to penetrate really deep, a rod as long as the Space Shuttle's cargo compartment, about 13.7 meters (45 feet), would have a diameter of 0.68 meter (2.25 ft), weigh 95,976 kg (211,148 lbs) and penetrate 41 meters (135 ft).

[66] Ibid.

armored vehicles,[67] extremely high velocities are not required. These lower velocities can allow the weapon to maneuver to attack moving targets, like surface ships or armored formations. Shortly before impact, the weapon would explode into a cloud of high-velocity projectiles. The detonation height and the projectiles would be optimized to achieve the desired effects against the type of target being attacked.

In addition to problems with orbital timing and responsiveness, precisely hitting a terrestrial target from orbit is far from simple. While it is probably feasible to hit a target as large as an armored formation with an area-type weapon when its location is precisely known, striking small, truly hard targets is far more difficult. Even assuming that the location of the target is precisely known, which is feasible for fixed targets, the weapon must be "aimed" accurately enough that atmospheric disturbances will not deflect it too severely. To aim the weapon it is necessary to release it at a very precise location and velocity. Great improvements in accuracy have been achieved for ICBM warheads, but while 100 meter accuracies are good enough for nuclear weapons; they are not nearly good enough for attacking hard targets with KE weapons.[68] Solving this problem will be essential if weapons moving at orbital velocities are to be used against very hard targets.

The conventional method for improving the accuracy of weapons, providing guidance and course corrections during the last seconds before impact, is not likely to work for high-speed orbital weapons. Even if a target could be "designated" with a laser, in which case conventional laser-guided weapons would probably be a more sensible choice, it would be difficult for a projectile moving at orbital speeds to "see" the laser early enough to make corrections. In fact, because of the plasma surrounding a weapon reentering the atmosphere at velocities in excess of 4.6 km/s,[69] it is unlikely that signals of any kind could reach the weapon. While adequate terminal guidance systems are

---

[67] Ibid.

[68] The accuracy of current U.S. ICBMs is reported to range from 90 meters circular error probable for the Peacekeeper to 120 meters for the Minuteman III. Lennox, Tab: Offensive Weapons, LGM-118 Peacekeeper and LGM 30G Minuteman III, Issue 26 January 1998.

[69] The Space Shuttle encounters a communications and telemetry blackout until it decelerates below 15,000 ft/s (4572 m/s) and descends below 180,000 ft. [W. Williamson et. al., "Technical Analysis of a Contingency Conventional Surgical Strike System," (Albuquerque, NM: Sandia National Laboratories, June 1995), 42. (Secret) Information extracted is unclassified.] It is reasonable to assume that guidance commands would also be blocked until these conditions are reached.

available for comparatively slow-speed weapons, those for orbital weapons travelling at 3 to 11 km/s will require significant improvements, such as ultra-precise inertial navigation units, before they can be considered feasible.

Common Aero Vehicle (CAV)

A concept that could solve some of the technical problems associated with orbital bombardment deals with the problem of high reentry velocities by using a maneuverable reentry vehicle. Deployed from an orbiting satellite, the weapon would slow from orbital speeds to speeds low enough to dispense conventional munitions. As it slowed, the weapon would be capable of aerodynamically maneuvering thousands of kilometers to either side of the orbital track without needing additional propellant.[70]

A weapon of this type has been proposed by the Armament Product Group at Eglin AFB Florida, and is called the Common Aero Vehicle (CAV). Air-launched sub-orbital missiles or ICBMs, as well as orbital platforms could deliver the CAV. If an orbital system were pursued, it would be possible to station large numbers of CAVs in LEO and de-orbit them when needed. With guidance, navigation and aerodynamic controls within the atmosphere, the CAV would dispense its submunitions at the appropriate geographic location. Prior to releasing them, the CAV would provide each individual submunition with target location coordinates.[71] The submunitions dispensed by the CAV would be optimized for force application missions, such as anti-armor, area denial, or hard-target penetration.[72] While the CAV overcomes the problem of accurately delivering weapons by slowing down and dispensing "smart" submunitions, it gives up the advantage of being able to hit hard targets at orbital velocities. This may be necessary given the state of current technology, however.

---

[70] Greg Jenkins, Office of the Armament Product Group Manager, Eglin AFB Florida. Briefing to the author, February 1998.
[71] Upon re-entry the CAV would determine guidance and navigation updates from either an inertial reference system (INS) closely coupled with the global positioning system (GPS) and/or an INS which uses stellar "fixes" for updates. [Ibid.]
[72] Ibid.

KE Weapons for Ballistic Missile Defense

Although directed energy weapons appear to have many properties desirable for BMD, their technological immaturity prompted the SDI program to start developing KE weapons to fill this role. The specific project initiated for this program, and continued for SDI's successor program, Global Protection Against Limited Strikes (GPALS), was Brilliant Pebbles.[73]

Brilliant Pebbles (BP) is a kinetic energy weapon system designed to defend against a ballistic missile attack. As envisioned for the GPALS concept, BP would consist of 700 to 1000 individual interceptors (small missiles called "pebbles") deployed into approximately 27 different orbits at an altitude of about 400 km (250 miles).[74] This deployment architecture would provide the capability to stop a limited strike of up to 200 missiles by destroying them during the boost phase of their flight.[75] It would be effective against all ballistic missiles except those with ranges less than 400-600 km or maximum altitudes lower than 80-100 km.[76]. Moving at about 5 miles/sec, the BP interceptors would destroy their targets by direct impact.

A system comprised of such a large number of individual interceptors requires a sophisticated system to control it. Two approaches to this problem have been proposed. The first is to design a system architecture that relies on cross-linking the individual interceptor satellites so that the ground control system is able to contact individual satellites and the satellites are able to communicate with each other. Cross-linking allows the majority of the computing power necessary for directing an attack to reside on the

---

[73] *United States General Accounting Office, Report to Chairman, Committee on Armed Services, U.S. Senate: Strategic Defense Initiative, Estimates of Brilliant Pebbles' Effectiveness Are Based on Many Unproven Assumptions*, GAO/NSIAD-92-91, (Washington, D.C.: General Accounting Office, 1992), 2.

[74] GAO/NSIAD-92-91, 8-10.

[75] Statement of Stephen J. Hadley, assistant secretary of defense for international security policy, quoted in William Matthews, "DOD restructuring SDI to fit a changing world," *Air Force Times*, 25 February 1991, 30.

[76] GAO/NSIAD-92-91, 15. Shorter range ballistic missiles do not leave the atmosphere, and due to problems similar to those encountered with orbital bombardment, the BP system is not designed to operate within it. Long-range missiles fired with depressed trajectories present similar problems since they do not leave the atmosphere until shortly before they burn out.

ground, an important consideration in a system that must simultaneously engage many targets without wasting multiple interceptors on any single one.

A less centralized approach is to give each interceptor almost total autonomy. With this design, the interceptors would be activated through a system of communication satellites, after which each one would determine which target to attack. As described by Lowell Wood of the Livermore Laboratory, "Each pebble would carry so much prior knowledge and detailed battle strategy and tactics, would compute so swiftly and would see so well that it could perform its purely defensive mission with no external supervision or coaching."[77] Aside from the moral reluctance of many to give any weapon so much autonomy, a major problem with this concept is to devise a computer/software combination that can do the job. To be practical, it must be cheap, small, require little power while it waits, and be "smart" enough to know which targets will be attacked by other pebbles and which target to attack itself. Even with the incredibly rapid progress being made in computer technology today, developing such a sophisticated computer small enough for missile guidance is unlikely to be possible for quite some time.

With an optimistically estimated cost of $55 billion (in 1988 dollars), Brilliant Pebbles was to be an extremely complex and very expensive system.[78] In addition to command and control, there were also significant technical challenges in building interceptors with the requisite speed, range and agility. These factors, coupled with a myriad of political considerations ranging from concerns about weaponizing space to the need to trim the budget, prompted Congress to cancel the program. Nevertheless, with further technological development, the concept behind Brilliant Pebbles has potential as either a BMD or ASAT system.

---

[77] Jonathan Jacky, "Throwing Stones at 'Brilliant Pebbles," *Technology Review*, 20 October 1989, 21.

[78] The General Accounting Office determined that the schedule upon which this cost estimate was based entailed a great deal of risk due to the highly concurrent nature of the development. It is reasonable to assume that had the system been pursued further, it would have cost considerably more than $55 billion. [*United States General Accounting Office, Report to the Chairman, Legislation and National Security Subcommittee, Committee on Government Operations, House of Representatives: Strategic Defense Initiative, Need to Examine Concurrency in Development of Brilliant Pebbles*, GAO/NSIAD-91-154, (Washington, D.C.: General Accounting Office, March 1991), 6.]

Weapons that Degrade Enemy Satellites

As an alternative to destruction, a target satellite may be captured or merely disabled, for instance by spraying paint on its solar cells or optical instruments. More sophisticated concepts involve disabling or degrading some critical sub-system of a target satellite, such as the attitude control system.

A potential advantage of weapons that degrade or disable enemy satellites is the possibility of using them covertly. The overall effect of doing this might extend far beyond the enemy's loss of the satellite. Surreptitiously disabling or degrading an enemy satellite could cause the enemy to waste valuable time reevaluating and possibly redesigning the "failed" satellite. As a minimum, the satellite will probably have to be replaced. In any case, unless the United States is at war with the other nation, any tampering with its satellites must be concealed…which makes this particularly attractive.

Depending on the overall strategy, the problems associated with this approach could be somewhat easier to solve than those of the space mine. If the weapon is to disable the target satellite immediately upon arrival, then there is no need for a long-term power source. This would permit the design of much smaller weapons that would be harder to detect, but would effectively be a ground-based system. If the weapon is not to be used immediately, i.e. is to be space-based, the problems with this concept would be similar to those of the space mine.

Defending Space-Based Assets

Unlike ground warfare, where the defense is normally thought to have the advantage, fighting a war in space is one in which the opposite is true. In space warfare, as in ground warfare, the attacker has the advantage of choosing the time, strength and direction of the attack. However the defender in space enjoys few of the advantages enjoyed by a land-based counterpart. Space has no terrain that can be prepared for defense, valuable assets cannot be dug-in and the enemy cannot be forced to attack from a specific direction. In sum, given an opponent with the capability to attack one's space-based assets, the defender is faced with a considerable dilemma.

The number of nations with the ability to develop weapons capable of attacking space-based assets, at least those in LEO, is increasing steadily. Direct ascent antisatellite weapons are well within the capabilities of any nation able to place a satellite in orbit, and possibly some capable of building only sounding rockets. Since a direct ascent ASAT does not have to achieve orbit, the booster to lift it can be relatively small and simple. In contrast to the boosters required to place a few hundred kilograms into orbit, one that only has to lift it a thousand kilometers weighs an order of magnitude less, only a few metric tons. This is within the capabilities of many sounding rockets developed by nations pursuing space-launch capabilities or large ballistic missiles. While a sophisticated KE ASAT would be out of reach even for many nations with the requisite boosters, a barrage of rockets fired into the path of a satellite and exploding into swarms of pellets could be effective. Given the relatively low cost of the boosters, this type of attack may be considered feasible by those nations possessing them.[79]

The ability to track satellites with precision is also necessary for a direct ascent ASAT. Unfortunately for the defender, this information is not difficult to come by. Organizations such as the Canadian Space Society routinely post the orbital elements of satellites on a computer bulletin board. These elements are determined through the observations of informal groups of satellite observers and may be accurate enough for a barrage type of attack. With a concerted effort a fairly simple tracking system could be developed to refine satellite tracking enough to greatly improve the probability of a barrage attack being effective.[80] While the low probability of kill achievable with this type of attack would never be good enough to satisfy the United States,[81] it presents too

---

[79] Allen Thomson, "Satellite vulnerability: a post-Cold War issue?" *Space Policy*, February 1995, 25.

[80] Ibid., 20-21.

[81] A barrage-type attack would require launching tens of rockets to achieve even a 50 percent probability of destroying a target. Since the United States would by definition be using an ASAT against another space-capable foe, the low odds coupled with the escalatory nature of such an attack would make it an untenable option. If the United States is going to run the risks of attacking satellites, then the decision makers will demand a virtual guarantee of success. Conversely, a nation that relies heavily on large, expensive, space-based assets cannot totally ignore even such a limited threat. However there are solutions that do not require space-based weapons. For a detailed review of what a low-tech adversary could accomplish against an enemy satellite, see Allen Thomson, "Satellite vulnerability: a post-Cold War issue?" *Space Policy*, February 1995.

much of a threat for the defender to ignore, particularly when that state depends heavily on space-based assets.

Bodyguards

One approach for defending satellites is the "bodyguard" concept. A bodyguard is a satellite that orbits near a high-value satellite and defends it against antisatellite weapons, including space mines.[82] These bodyguards could be designed around either directed energy or physical impact weapons. While the idea of stationing a defensive weapon near a satellite seems logical at first glance, its problems actually mirror those inherent in the offensive ASAT systems discussed above.

When designing a bodyguard, it is first necessary to determine what type of threat it will defend against, and how much cueing information will be provided by off-board sensors. If it is not feasible for the United States to deploy space-based ASATs, then it is arguably just as infeasible for a prospective adversary to do so. This assumption would limit the problem, since only ground-based ASATs would need to be defended against. Couple this with the fact that the United States already has the capability to track any boosters launched from the surface of the earth, and the capabilities required for a bodyguard drop dramatically. Launch warning and booster tracking would make attacks on satellites difficult to conceal, although a determined foe might realize this and pursue orbital ASATs regardless of their other drawbacks. An additional tactic would be for an adversary to launch an ASAT into an orbit that appeared to have no relation to the target, for instance a geosynchronous transfer orbit, and then have the ASAT change orbits later in its trajectory. While such an approach would entail a much more sophisticated weapon and a much larger booster, a peer competitor could realistically build such a system. Unless the United States begins carefully evaluating the potential for this type of attack

---

[82] "Air Force 2025 in detail: Part II AF worries that space mines may threaten future ops," *Military Space* 13, No. 23, 11 November 1996, 7.

and closely tracks all maneuvers enemy satellites make once they are on orbit,[83] this type of attack could approach a target from any direction with little warning. For the purposes of this analysis, it is assumed that these steps are taken and that a bodyguard system would know the direction and time of any attacks.

The high-energy laser may at first appear to be an excellent candidate for the job of bodyguard. Unfortunately, designing a laser for bodyguard work presents more problems than does using lasers as ASAT or BMD weapons. Since the orbits of potential targets are well known before an ASAT is even launched, and for BMD a network of sensors need only focus on the earth and detect very bright and relatively slow-moving targets, these missions are somewhat easier.[84] In contrast, bodyguards must be effective against ASATs that may be either moderately easy to see and very fast moving (relative velocities of 20+ km/s) in the case of KE ASATs, or very slow moving and very difficult to detect, for space mines.

To be effective, HEL bodyguards must be optimized for ranges almost as long as those needed for BMD. Even with a relatively slow closing velocity of 4 km/s, a laser would need to engage the ASAT at a range of 1,000 km just to allow sufficient time (250 seconds) for damage assessment and for the protected asset to make a modest maneuver to avoid the disabled ASAT by a safe margin. Admittedly, the vastness of space makes an ASAT achieving a kill without terminal guidance unlikely, but prudence would likely dictate that the protected asset be maneuvered in order to be sure of avoiding destruction. (Given a sophisticated ASAT, avoidance maneuvers made before it was disabled would be futile since the ASAT could compensate for them.) Assuming this nominal range of 1,000 km, the greatest drawback of a DE bodyguard is probably its cost. With performance requirements close to those of a BMD system, and given the near-term state of the art, a HEL based bodyguard might cost far more than the satellite being defended.

---

[83] It is apparent from descriptions of the U.S. system that the detailed tracking necessary to counter attacks by a determined foe will not be possible without substantial steps being taken bolster current capabilities. [Michael J. Muolo, *Space Handbook: An Analyst's Guide, Volume One*, (Maxwell AFB, Ala.: Air University Press, December 1993), 74-84.]

[84] Although ballistic missiles reach high velocities at burnout, they initially start from rest and provide a very bright source infrared source for a period of at least a minute.

Other directed energy weapons, like radio frequency weapons, could also theoretically perform the bodyguard function. However a problem with these weapons is the difficulty in determining when the ASAT has been "killed." Since the weapons only disrupt the electronics of the ASAT there may be no way to know if the defense was effective. Another problem is that disrupting the ASAT's electronics might not change its orbit, which may already be an intercept trajectory. Similar to the HEL bodyguard, the asset may have to be moved just to be on the safe side. Another drawback to an RF bodyguard is that an enemy ASAT will probably be shielded from all but the strongest RF attacks. For these reasons it is unlikely that RF weapons will be actively considered for the bodyguard role.

Considering the needed performance capabilities, KE-based bodyguards will also be expensive. Against fast-moving KE ASATs, both good sensors and high maneuverability would be necessary. As with DE weapons, a KE bodyguard intercepting a KE ASAT faces the same challenges as do KE ASATs themselves. It may not need to constantly scan for hostile satellites if it can depend on an overarching detection system, but it must be able to track the ASAT far enough away to make interception possible. Given the nature of orbital dynamics and KE ASATs, it will be most effective to intercept the ASAT a long distance from the protected asset (to minimize the chance that debris generated by the interception will finish the ASAT's job). Intercepting a fast-moving satellite at long ranges dictates a very large weapon with a large amount of ΔV available.[85] In light of these facts, a bodyguard designed to counter a KE ASAT will probably look much like its nemesis, but must be able to react and travel much faster.

Assuming a robust space tracking system, the most common threats should be fairly easy to defend against. These threats are the direct ascent ASAT, the co-orbital ASAT, and to a lesser extent the space mine. A direct-ascent ASAT is one that is launched from the earth directly into the path of the target. It is a KE weapon that uses

---

[85] "ΔV available" is a direct measure of the ability of a satellite to change its orbit. Large orbit changes require large ΔVs, for instance changing the inclination of a satellite in a 400-km altitude orbit by ninety degrees (an admittedly extreme change) requires a ΔV greater than the existing orbital speed. Intercepting an ASAT that is approaching at an angle of ninety degrees will likely require even more energy and an improbable amount of lead-time. [Muolo, *Space Handbook Vol. Two*, p 70)

the velocity differential, in excess of 8 km/s, to destroy the target. These weapons are usually considered to be effective only against satellites in low-earth orbit, since attacking satellites in higher orbits would require an inordinately large booster. A direct-ascent ASAT does not actually enter orbit, and by its nature must be firing its booster almost until interception. Since these ASATs must be launched from almost directly underneath the orbital path and shortly before the target satellite is overhead, the problem of detecting the ASAT and training a weapon on it is considerably reduced. A bodyguard satellite could be similar to a Brilliant Pebbles interceptor, with considerably reduced requirements regarding the number of sensors, their field of view, the range of the interceptor, and the complexity of the control system. In essence all that would be needed is relatively simple system to scan the earth in front of the satellite and along its direction of travel. This sensor would be coupled to a very fast missile having a range of several hundred kilometers (as opposed to thousands for BMD).

The co-orbital ASAT is another threat that would be relatively easy to defend against. Since launch detection and trajectory tracking would provide warning of an impending attack, the bodyguard could be oriented in the proper direction without the need to do its own scanning. Once the target was acquired, the same type of interceptor used against a direct ascent ASAT could be launched at the co-orbital weapon. Defending against a co-orbital attack would be far less demanding than the direct ascent attack since the relative velocities would be much slower and any system designed for the latter should be more than adequate for the former.

The space mine may present greater challenges to an orbital bodyguard. If space mines can be designed to be stealthy, including virtually eliminating their infrared signature, then a major problem with defending against them may be detecting their presence. Detecting a satellite that is trying to stealthily close with the protected asset requires sensors that can scan in virtually all directions. The sensors must also be equally good at detecting infrared sources against the cold background of space as well as the much warmer background of the earth. While these capabilities may make a bodyguard somewhat more complicated than one only effective against non-stealth ASATs, the problems are likely not insurmountable. If it can be detected, the space mine should be fairly easy to neutralize.

The biggest potential drawback for a bodyguard is the likely cost of such a system. While it would probably be most efficient for a bodyguard to have a service life comparable to that of the asset being protected, this requirement dictates a very capable weapon that can withstand years of inactivity with no maintenance and still reliably accomplish its mission. Even deploying enough of them to defend only military satellites would be expensive; deploying enough to defend civilian satellites as well would be cost-prohibitive.[86]

To summarize, the bodyguard concept suffers from most of the same problems as do the weapons it is intended to protect against. In addition, the bodyguard has the disadvantage of being purely defensive, although it would have at least some offensive ASAT capabilities. Being defensive, the bodyguard system would have to be able to detect, track, intercept and destroy an enemy ASAT with advance warning consisting of little more than the general direction in which direct its sensors. A system with these capabilities probably can be constructed, but it will not be cheap.

Other Concepts for Defending Space-Based Assets

Alternatives to bodyguards include derivatives of both BMD and ASAT concepts. The most notable of these are ground-based lasers to destroy enemy ASATs, which will be discussed in Chapter 3, and the previously discussed space-based BMD system which could prevent an enemy from launching any satellites at all. Other concepts such as counter-ASATs, either KE or explosive, would in essence be the bodyguards just described. Regardless of which concept proves to be most promising, each would rely on an extensive surveillance system of some kind, either self-contained or deployed separately.

---

[86] While the number of low-altitude military satellites is fairly limited today, a trend towards larger numbers of smaller satellites in lower orbits would drive up the costs of protecting them. If civilian satellites are to be defended, then the numbers are already prohibitive since five communications networks alone are in the process of launching a total of more than 500 satellites into LEO. [John V. Evans, "New Satellites for Personal Communications," *Scientific American*, April 1998, 72-3.]

Technological Factors Bearing on Space-Based Weapons

Surveillance for Space Control

If a system to defend satellites is to be fielded, then it will probably require a space-based surveillance system in order to provide continuous protection. While relying on current systems for launch detection and trajectory tracking may be adequate, there remains the possibility of an a enemy ASAT making large orbital changes while it is out of sight of the current U.S. surveillance system. One option for correcting this potential shortfall would be to bolster the current U.S. ground-based surveillance system. Unfortunately if such a system is to provide continuous coverage for all U.S. satellites, then this approach requires a worldwide network of ground stations. Obtaining these ground stations could prove to be problematic.

Another option is some sort of space-based surveillance system, but developing such a system would be a major endeavor. While the U.S. possesses space-based systems to warn against missile launches and nuclear detonations, space-based systems to monitor satellites in orbit have not yet been built. Such a system would have to deal with a much more diverse array of targets, and survey a much larger volume of space than do current systems. If the system were comprised of a network of cross-linked surveillance satellites, a large number of ground stations would not be necessary; however such a space-based system may itself need protection. Regardless of which method is used, a surveillance system effective against space mines must be capable of detecting small, stealthy satellites at great ranges.

Since ASAT weapons deployed in space (particularly space mines) would be fairly small and have relatively weak infrared signatures; any *passive* surveillance system will require large numbers of satellites in a variety of orbits. An approach using *active* surveillance systems such as radar may require fewer satellites; however each one will require large amounts of power and still may be defeated by stealthy ASAT weapons. Regardless of the approach taken, a system designed for space surveillance would probably have to be deployed in multiple, non-geosynchronous orbits to provide adequate coverage. Using multiple orbits would considerably increase the complexity and cost of the system. While the technical difficulties associated with such a system pale in comparison to those of the space-based weapons themselves, it would still constitute a large additional expense. However if a satellite defense is to be effective against a determined peer competitor, it will require a more comprehensive surveillance system than is available today.

System architecture

Until now this discussion has focused on the types of space-based weapons that have been proposed, their potential capabilities, and the technological challenges that must be overcome to make them feasible. What has not been discussed, and what has been neglected in virtually all discussions of space-based weapons, are the steps that must be taken to knit these different weapons into a robust system.

Ideally, a system architecture will ensure that the space-based weapons are used in a mutually supporting and coordinated manner. It will have to include a tracking and targeting system that can determine information such as how quickly a target must be destroyed, and which satellite or method of intercept will have the highest probability of kill. This information must then be fused and presented in such a manner that a decision-maker can quickly select the optimum response. The vast number of variables involved may well argue for a computer to make the decision. This alone would entail a whole new discussion about the desirability of letting a computer decide to employ weapons.[87]

While the computer and communication technology needed for an effective command and control system is advancing much more rapidly than is the development of orbital weapons, the cost of the requisite system, as well as its vulnerabilities, will weigh heavily in any decision to deploy space-based weapons.

---

[87] One barrier to giving computers the ability to fire weapons is a law passed by Congress. This law stipulates that "No agency of the Federal government may pay for, fund, or otherwise support the development of command and control systems for strategic defense in the boost or post-boost phase against ballistic missile threats that would permit such strategic defense to initiate the directing of damaging or lethal fire except by affirmative human discretion at an appropriate level of authority." [National Defense Authorization Act for FY 1988-89, H.R. 1748, Division A, Title II, Part C, Subpart 1, Section 224.]

Cost and Responsiveness of Space Lift

Perhaps the most important economic factor affecting the decision to deploy space-based weapons is the cost and availability of space lift. This is particularly true of systems requiring large constellations of satellites, like Brilliant Pebbles. Launch costs currently range from about $4,300/lb for a Delta II to $10,000/lb for the space shuttle,[88] and comprise 25 to 30 percent of a satellite's total cost.[89] Reducing them by half, the target for the Evolved Expendable Launch Vehicle (EELV)[90] would greatly improve the affordability of space-based weapons. Reducing launch costs by a factor of 10, the goal of many new launch concepts, NASA's X-33 program being the most prominent, could radically alter the economics of space-based weapons.[91]

Another facet of operating in space is achieving routine access. Routine access entails the ability to launch and/or recover multiple spacecraft in a manner and with a regularity similar to that enjoyed by aircraft. While closely related to cost, routine access requires a robust and redundant launch system that may entail large investments. This investment will be necessary if space-based weapons systems requiring large constellations of satellites are to be deployed. Systems such as a Brilliant Pebbles-type ballistic missile defense will need to launch many replacement satellites for those that malfunction or reach the end of their service life. Fortunately, the ever-increasing rate of

---

[88] These figures are in 1993 dollars. [John R. London III, *LEO on the Cheap*, (Maxwell AFB, AL: Air University Press, 1994), 5.] More recently, Daniel Goldin, the NASA Administrator, confirms a cost of 10,000 $/lb for the shuttle. [Peter Spiegel, "Free Launch?" *Forbes*, 24 February 1997, 76.]

[89] The SDIO projected the launch costs of Brilliant Eyes, the sensors that were to cue the Brilliant Pebbles weapons, to be 25 percent of total life-cycle cost. [John R. London III, *LEO on the Cheap*, (Maxwell AFB, AL: Air University Press, 1994), 1.] Similarly Motorola estimates launch costs to comprise about 30 percent of the total cost of its Iridium communications satellite constellation. [G. Harry Stine, "Opening the Spaceways," *Barron's*, 19 May 1997, 62.]

[90] Joseph C. Anselmo and Bruce A. Smith, "Cost Drives EELV," *Aviation Week and Space Technology*, 6 January 1997, 27.

[91] NASA Administrator Daniel Goldin cited a 10-fold reduction launch costs as the target for the X-33 program. [Spiegel, 23-4.] Alternatively Kistler Aerospace estimates launch costs of 2,000 $/lb for LEO launches on a vehicle designed to use off-the-shelf components. [Joseph C. Anselmo, "Launchers See Nothing But Blue Skies Ahead," *Aviation Week & Space Technology*, 7 April 1997, 41.] For a discussion of the military implications of reduced launch costs, see William W. Bruner III, "National Security Implications of Inexpensive Space Access," Master's thesis, School of Advanced Airpower Studies, Maxwell AFB, AL, June 1995).

commercial space launches is prompting a rapid growth in companies offering launch services. The boosters these companies develop could also be used for military launches, although there is currently such a backlog of satellites waiting to be launched that the system is far from responsive.[92]

The peacetime demand for launching and replacing orbital weapons will most likely increase in the event of hostilities. This alone may dictate an increased ability to launch large numbers of spacecraft quickly. If an enemy should develop the capability to strike U.S. launch facilities with space-based weapons of his own, the need for a robust launch system is even more obvious.

This last concern brings out an aspect of the launch cost and access problem that may not be readily apparent. While the advantages of reduced cost and increased space access for the United States are obvious, the options this will give potential adversaries may be equally important. As the technology necessary for cheap and routine access to space proliferates, more nations will be able to launch their own satellites and hence their own space-based weapons.

---

[92] Arianspace is forecasting $30-40 billion of spacecraft launches over the next decade, excluding military. Also, according to John Perkins, vice president of launch services for Hughes Telecommunications & Space, capacity of industry to produce satellites "far outstrips global launch capacity." [Anselmo, "Launchers See Nothing But Blue Skies Ahead," 42.]

Summary

As U.S. national leaders ponder the wisdom of placing weapons in orbit, it is necessary to determine what these weapons can be expected to do. This chapter has attempted to lay out the potential capabilities and limitations of space-based weapons. At this point some tentative conclusions suggest themselves.

Lasers have been proposed as ideal weapons for both space control and boost-phase ballistic missile defense. Their primary advantage is a laser's ability to strike in any direction at the speed of light. Unfortunately, they have major limitations in terms of the power levels available with current technology, the need for large quantities of chemical fuel, and the enormous space structures needed to support them.

Kinetic energy and co-orbital weapons have also been proposed for space control and ballistic missile defense, but are not without problems of their own. These include timing constraints placed upon them by orbital mechanics, the vast distances that must be covered to reach a target, and the large amounts of propellant needed to make all but the simplest attack.

Bombardment weapons that exploit the kinetic energy inherent in orbital weapons have considerable potential, but require improvements in precision guidance and warhead materials to be widely useful. A partial solution to this problem may be a concept such as the Common Aero Vehicle, but a major selling point of orbital weapons, their high impact velocity and its potential effectiveness against deeply buried hardened targets, is sacrificed in order to achieve greater precision against softer targets. However, given the limitations of currently available materials, this may not be a significant loss.

Finally, this brief analysis indicates that defending satellites is at least as difficult as attacking them. The bodyguard concept looks good at first glance, but actually entails all of the problems of conventional ASATs with the added need to be able to react to attacks with minimal warning. Bodyguard satellites *would* force effective ASATs to be more sophisticated and minimize threats from enemies other than peer competitors, but a decision to deploy these weapons must take their costs and limitations into consideration.

Chapter 3

Seeking Control of Space: Ground-Based Alternatives for Space Control

The United States has become highly dependent on space-based assets. The space-control mission seeks to protect these assets and deny an enemy access to space. Many of the orbital space control weapons were outlined in the previous chapter. Most of the missions these weapons would be capable of doing could also be accomplished by either surface-based or airborne systems. The purpose of this chapter is to compare space-based weapons with these alternatives.

Defensive Counterspace

Maintaining access to space requires that all parts of a complex system be protected. The main components of this system are the satellites themselves, the ground stations that control them, and any mobile ground stations capable of receiving satellite generated data. The latter range from handheld "cell phones" to tactical terminals capable of receiving satellite imagery. Each of these components, as well as the communication links between them, are susceptible to attack. Protecting this system is the essence of Defensive Counterspace.

Probably the most vulnerable part of the system is the network of ground stations. Given the fact that they are relatively few in number and are "soft" targets with known locations, attacks against ground stations should be expected in the event of war.[93] While it is possible to deploy mobile ground stations, using them will almost certainly degrade

---

[93] For example the U.S. system is comprised of three space operations centers located in the United States and nine remote tracking stations scattered around the world. [Michael J. Muolo, *Space Handbook, A War Fighter's Guide to Space, Volume One*, (Maxwell AFB, Ala.: Air University Press, December 1993), 75-9.]

the efficiency of the system.[94] Equally vulnerable are the facilities needed to launch satellites into orbit. Although they are somewhat more difficult to destroy, the need to defend launch facilities is potentially greater since they are fewer in number and making them mobile is extremely difficult. As potentially critical as these vulnerabilities may be, defending them is more a matter for conventional security arrangements than space-based assets. However, it is important to note that any investments made in space-based weapons would be wasted if the ground stations needed to make use of them were neutralized. Aside from this rather critical point, defending ground stations will not be discussed any further here.

Protection Through Redundancy

Until very recently, U.S. satellites have tended to be fairly large, very capable and very expensive. These satellites present an opponent with lucrative targets, where the loss of even one would often constitute a dramatic loss in capability. This is particularly true for current generation reconnaissance satellites since these are very capable, relatively few in number, and very vulnerable owing to their need to be in low earth orbits. Fortunately deploying defensive space weapons is only one way to protect these assets.

One option for mitigating this vulnerability is to deploy large numbers of less capable satellites. These satellites could provide the same capability as a larger satellite by working in concert. For a satellite communication system, each satellite would carry part of the load. If needed, the satellites could be placed fairly close together in orbit and their deployment geometry could be optimized to balance survivability with the need to emulate a much more capable satellite. Alternatively, the U.S. could move away from placing communication satellites in geosynchronous orbit and transition to a large constellation of satellites in lower orbits. The commercial sector is now using such an approach to provide global cellular telephone capability.

---

[94] In order to be mobile, a ground station would have to rely on communication links that are also mobile. This virtually rules out the use of land communications with their high bandwidth and resistance to jamming. Mobile systems would probably rely on microwave or radio communications which not only carry less information, but are more

Reconnaissance satellites could also be designed as a distributed network. Experiments conducted by the Clementine spacecraft demonstrated that even very small and inexpensive satellites could collect militarily useful data.[95] While the highest resolution imagery may still require large satellites, a network of small satellites could meet many needs and would provide graceful degradation in the event one is lost. In contrast to the loss of a single highly capable satellite, which could be crippling, the remaining satellites in a network would still provide significant capability. With total costs on the order of only 12 percent of that of large satellites, small satellites seem to be the next logical step.[96]

Rapid Reconstitution

An additional step that can be taken to assure access to space is to develop a responsive space-lift capability. The ability to prepare and launch a satellite within days could quickly replenish combat losses. This approach would be most cost-effective for small, cheap satellites, but would also be effective for larger satellites, particularly if an enemy had only a limited number of ASAT weapons. Spares that are stored on the ground until needed would offer more than just the ability to replenish combat losses quickly. Since they would be accessible while in storage, ground spares could be upgraded so that they incorporate the latest technology when they are eventually

---

susceptible to interference. Other losses in efficiency may be caused by the need to periodically move the station in order to prevent its discovery and destruction.

[95] Clementine incorporated seven sensors, along with the attitude control, power, and the computer systems required to control and point them, for a total dry weight of only 500 lbs. Its Lidar High Resolution Camera weighed only 1250 grams and produced images with a resolution equivalent to 6 meters from a distance of 380 km. [Pedro L. Rustan, "Clementine Test Results," Unpublished research results, Ballistic Missile Defense Organization, The Pentagon, Washington D.C.: 31 October 1994, 1.; and U.S. Naval Research Laboratory, *Moonglow*, (Washington D.C.: Naval Research Laboratory, June 1994), 28.]

[96] As an example: A constellation of 143 satellites, weighing 100 kg and operating in 367 km orbits, provides the same coverage and resolution as a constellation of 4 satellites, weighing 10,000 kg and operating at 3666 km. Each of these would meet the need for 10 percent instantaneous global coverage at a resolution of 1 meter (or equivalently, 1 m resolution of a given point on earth for 10 percent of the time). The importance of this is that 100 kg satellites can do the same job for only 12 percent of the cost of the larger satellites. [Michael R. Stamm, "How Technology is Changing the Optimum Size of Satellites," Unpublished Research Paper, Phillips Laboratory, Kirtland AFB, NM: December 1994, 67-70.]

launched. The DSP satellite program made use of this concept in the 1980s, when unneeded spare satellites were upgraded to become more capable replacements.[97] Designing spare satellites to allow for upgrades would capitalize on their availability during storage, an attribute that makes such a strategy even more attractive than attempting to actively defend obsolescing hardware in orbit.

The United States is already pursuing several concepts that seek to exploit responsive launch capability. One employs relatively small tactical reconnaissance satellites that would be deployed by a re-useable space plane. The satellite/space plane combination would have a life span of about a year in orbit and the ability to make orbital plane changes of up to 20 degrees. This maneuverability provides the capability to alter orbits to meet mission requirements while the concept as a whole would allow the satellite to be recovered along with the space plane. The fact that the tactical satellites would only be deployed in the event of war coupled with their considerable ability to maneuver, would make these satellites difficult for an adversary to track and engage.

The defensive measures just discussed seek to assure access to space through essentially passive means. The space-based assets are not defended, but instead are made resistant to attack. While these approaches might not provide as much protection as a *truly effective* defensive system, creating such a defensive system is problematic. The approaches outlined above would, on the other hand, assure continued use of space-based assets in the event of attack, and present an adversary seeking to attack them with a much greater challenge. These approaches should also be much cheaper than space-based weapons, and may in fact be all that is needed.

Active Defense

If it is determined that passive measures will not provide adequate protection for space-based assets, more active methods are available. As outlined in Chapter 2, the only method that appears to be feasible is a bodyguard concept for use against direct-ascent and co-orbital ASATs. While the Brilliant Pebbles concept for BMD has the potential to

---

[97] J. Cushman, "To Detect ICBM Launch, AF Seeks Invulnerable Warning Satellites," *Defense Week*, January 16 1984, p 1, 10.

be effective in this role, its high cost is only one of the factors that make it a controversial proposition.

A potentially less controversial, and less expensive, method of defending space-based assets is to attack the enemy's ASAT capability on the ground. Similar in concept to an offensive counterair strategy, such an approach is well founded in airpower doctrine. When applied to the satellite defense problem, attacking ASAT weapons on the ground is even less complicated. Whereas combat aircraft are normally dispersed to many airfields in time of war, ASATs will be restricted to relatively few easily identifiable launch sites. Once hostilities begin, these sites will be open to attacks by conventional assets such as stealth aircraft and cruise missiles.

An additional point about passive defense bears consideration. While nuclear weapons are not a primary focus of this paper, rapid reconstitution may be the best way to overcome the effects of a high-altitude nuclear detonation.[98] While the international political repercussions may prevent most potential adversaries from using nuclear weapons even in space, there are those who may not be dissuaded. If one of these nations develops and uses nuclear ASATs, space-based defensive weapons may be of little use. The ability to quickly reconstitute space-based assets may well be the only practical solution.

Offensive Counterspace

Space-based anti-satellite weapons have the potential to deny an enemy the use of his space-based systems. As outlined previously, these concepts are expensive and pose many technical challenges. Alternatives to space-based weapons have the potential to be equally effective, more flexible, more technologically feasible and less expensive.

---

[98] The effects of a high-altitude nuclear detonation include an electromagnetic pulse (EMP) produced during the detonation and the creation of large quantities of charged particles that can become trapped in the Earth's radiation belts. The EMP can damage or destroy the electronic components of unhardened satellites that are within line-of-sight of a detonation, and even hardened satellites can be rendered inoperative for days or weeks due to the effects of either the EMP or the charged particles.

Non-Destructive Approaches to Offensive Counterspace

Diplomacy

The least expensive approach to denying an enemy access to space is only practical against nations that rely on leasing third-party assets. This has the potential to become prevalent as commercial enterprises devoted to providing communications and surveillance become more common. In these situations, it may be possible to convince the corporations or nations providing the service to cut off access during a conflict. In fact doing much more may be politically unfeasible, since direct attacks would be difficult to justify even if it could be proven that a corporation was providing an adversary with satellite support. Unfortunately diplomatic pressure may not be effective since corporations will stand to lose customers if they cannot be relied upon in emergencies. This approach also requires the United States to have considerable international support and would be problematic in situations where the United States is acting unilaterally.[99]

Non-Destructive Jamming

A more practical approach to denying an enemy use of his space-based assets may be to jam the communication links between the satellites and the ground stations. Since this approach would not damage the satellites, the fact that they may be owned by third parties would be less of a factor. Jamming the communications between satellites and

---

[99] The potential problems with a diplomatic approach were highlighted during the Gulf War of 1991. The Iraqi government had been buying satellite imagery from the French company SPOT Image prior to the war, but international condemnation of Iraqi actions prompted the company to cut off access. SPOT Image also refused to provide imagery to television and other media organizations, thus preventing Iraq from gathering the information from these sources. A potential shortcoming of this approach is illustrated by the fact that SPOT Image retained the option of selling imagery to the media if another source started doing so. In fact, the Earth Observation Satellite Co. (EOSAT) did start selling imagery to the media, although it was prohibited from selling directly to Iraq by the U.S. embargo. Fortunately the images available from EOSAT were of a lower resolution than those produced by SPOT (30 m vs 10 m) and SPOT Image held to its initial decision. [Peter B. DeSelding and Andrew Lawler, "SPOT Halts Sales of Gulf Area Imagery," *Space News*, August 13-19, 1990, 3. Renee Saunders, "Eosat Sees High Demand for Gulf Images," *Space News*, September 24-30, 1990, 3.] For a more

their ground stations may prove difficult because the large antennas used by ground stations are highly directional and jamming them could require inordinate amounts of power. An additional problem would be positioning the jamming platform within line-of-sight of the target ground station. Such an approach would be contingent on having total air supremacy, a condition that may not always prevail. Some satellite-dependent communication systems, on the other hand, are easier to jam. These systems rely on lower power, non-directional antennas on the ground, and sensitive receivers on the satellite. Operational problems with current satellite communication systems indicate that high power jamming of a satellite may be sufficient to block communications.[100]

An important objective of most conflicts has been disrupting the enemy's command and control system. In conventional wars against small, less sophisticated enemies (for instance Iraq) it has usually been easy to do this. New developments in communications may make this more difficult in the future. Cellular telephone systems with global coverage are now being built. These systems use large constellations of satellites in low orbit to carry phone calls around the world.[101] A relatively small nation, such as Iraq, could easily purchase enough capacity on these systems to provide military communications throughout its country. While such a service would be expensive, it would cost much less than building an entire satellite communication system. The problems it creates for any country attempting to disrupt this type of communication system may make it a particularly attractive option.

When attempting to disrupt an enemy's command and control network, it would be problematic for the United States to destroy the third-party commercial satellites that comprise it. Destroying all of the satellites would not only be very expensive in terms of

---

thorough discussion of this topic, see Cynthia A. S. McKinley, "When the Enemy Has Our Eyes," (Maxwell AFB, Ala: School of Advanced Airpower Studies, June 1995).

[100] Development of the C-17 SATCOM communication equipment showed that even an authorized user transmitting at an unauthorized high power level effectively blocked-out users with the standard low power transmitters. While this problem has been addressed, the high-power transmitters in question were not designed as jammers. Equipment specifically designed to jam this system would likely be even more effective. [Personal experience in the C-17 System Program Office.]

[101] The system nearest to deployment will begin service late in 1998 and employs 66 satellites. Called "Iridium" the system has 51 satellites in orbit as of March 1998. [Michael A. Dornheim, "Vandenberg Launches Eight Satellites," *Aviation Week and Space Technology*, February 23 1998, 41.]

the weapons required, the corporations owning the satellites and the other nations of the world would probably condemn such actions. While the United States could ignore international opinion if the cause were important enough, a less controversial solution would be preferable. Ideally it would be possible to persuade the corporation running the system to deactivate service to an opponent, but this may not always be the case. The best method for disrupting these communications may prove to be conventional jamming of the hand-held phones the field commanders would be using. While this is not a very elegant solution, it may be the

only feasible one since any large-scale interference with a satellite-based telephone system would have global repercussions.

If an adversary owns and maintains its own space-based assets, then the United States would have freer reign in disrupting them. One method would be to prevent the satellites from receiving commands from the ground. While jamming the large, highly directional antennas of the ground stations might be difficult, the antennas on the satellites themselves are much more vulnerable. The results of jamming these signals would vary from slow degradation of the orbit, to disrupting satellite communication networks, to preventing reconnaissance satellites from being tasked. This latter effect may be useful, but its effectiveness would be difficult to verify, since it might not be obvious that a reconnaissance satellite is no longer performing its mission.

Another type of jamming is possible against reconnaissance satellites that take visual or infrared pictures. This non-destructive concept would make use of portable devices that track a satellite while it is overhead and train a laser on it. Experiments have shown that even low-power lasers can temporarily blind optical sensors.[102] The simplicity and low power requirements of these systems are such that they could easily be deployed on small vehicles and, with further development, could be made man-portable.

---

[102] Even relatively low-power lasers have demonstrated the capability to damage the optical sensors of satellites. A test was conducted which directed a 30 watt laser at an orbiting test satellite (the test was supposed to be made with the 2 megawatt MIRACL laser but it malfunctioned). Even such a low powered laser caused enough damage to create "a lot of panic" in the Pentagon. [Bill Gertz, "Shared satellite laser test weighed," *The Washington Times*, Friday January 2 1998.] In a related area, the Starfire optical range at the Philips Laboratory used a tracking system constructed from an Atari

The drawback of this approach is similar to that of jamming command signals: its effectiveness would be very difficult to verify. Since it would not be possible to tell if a satellite was actually blinded, there would be no way to determine that the enemy remained unaware of troop dispositions or whatever other information was to be denied him.

In spite of the drawbacks, using lasers to temporarily blind reconnaissance or surveillance satellites has the potential to deny an enemy the use of third-party satellites without unduly antagonizing the third party. One strategy may be to declare a total exclusion zone over the theater of operations and give warning that any satellites over-flying the region would be liable to engagement by potentially damaging lasers. It would then be the responsibility of the satellite's owner to ensure that the satellite was oriented so as to protect its sensors. In a variation of this approach, small satellites could be built to rendezvous with the satellite in question and verify that the satellite was indeed pointed away from the area of concern. While such an approach may not be able to determine if a non-cooperative satellite was damaged by a subsequent laser engagement, complaints of satellite damage from the satellite's owner could provide the required feedback.

Rather than jamming, a potentially more effective approach may be to take command of a problem satellite. It may be possible to break the codes used to command the maneuvers of a satellite and send it spurious instructions. If transmitters were placed so that they could overpower legitimate commands, or send commands when the legitimate transmitters are out of range, then a satellite could be prevented from performing its mission. In contrast to jamming a satellite, the reactions of the satellite would make it possible to verify that the attack had been successful.

Another alternative along these lines is to develop a satellite capable of physically moving an uncooperative satellite. Such devices have been proposed for regaining control of malfunctioning satellites that are trapped in useless orbits or not responding to maneuver commands. The same device could be used to disrupt control of a third-party or enemy satellite by maneuvering it so that it could not take pictures of the designated

---

computer and electronic parts available at retail outlets. [Maj Mark Jelonek (Ph.D., laser physics) Interviewed by the author, 12 May 1998.]

area. If the satellite's owners were unable to monitor other spacecraft in orbit, then this assault could well be made surreptitiously.

Alternatives to physically destroying an enemy's space-based assets offer the least controversial approaches to denying an enemy access to space. From diplomatic efforts with third party providers, to jamming command and control links, non-destructive methods have the potential to be both effective and inexpensive. These approaches would be most effective against a less capable foe, while a peer competitor may have the ability to counter them. Considering the potential implications of an enemy's unhindered access to space, it is also prudent to also consider more definitive measures for space control.

Destructive Approaches to Offensive Counterspace

While non-destructive approaches to space control have considerable potential, circumstances may dictate more violent measures. The least technologically challenging destructive approach is to destroy the ground stations needed to communicate with satellites. This method is similar to the jamming options discussed above in that it attacks the communication links that make space-based assets useful. Relatively large, fixed ground stations are necessary both to control satellites and to receive the information they are gathering. While the potential exists to develop mobile ground stations, most systems in use today rely on stations whose locations are known with a high degree of accuracy. These ground stations are soft targets that are extremely vulnerable to either sabotage or conventional attack by systems currently in the inventory.

The effects of attacking ground stations would be very similar to those of jamming. While the destruction of the ground station would be readily apparent, the possibility would exist that an as yet undiscovered ground station would take over the function of the one destroyed. As with jamming, changes in the behavior of the satellite might not be great enough to confirm the effectiveness of the attack. It is for these reasons that many ASAT advocates decry the efficacy of this approach.[103] Even if a

---

[103] Not surprisingly, mobile ground stations are cited as a justification for building the KE ASAT by the contractor team developing the weapon. ["Kinetic Energy Anti-Satellite Program (KE ASAT) Background and Overview," briefing by Rockwell Corp and

future adversary develops mobile ground stations, it is unlikely that they will be as capable as the fixed stations, the destruction of which will thus degrade the usefulness of the space-based assets.

Destroying Adversaries' Space-Based Assets

The most certain method of denying an enemy the use of his space-based assets is to physically destroy the satellites themselves. Doing this from the ground makes use of the same principles as the space-based methods discussed in the preceding chapter. Ground-based directed energy weapons, KE ASATs, and co-orbital ASATs are the three major types of weapons.

Ground-based lasers seem to offer many advantages over their space-based counterparts. In addition to not needing to withstand long-term storage in space, the availability of large supplies of chemical fuel and the lack of constraints on their size make ground-based lasers much more practical. A problem with ground basing is that the Earth's atmosphere tends to absorb laser energy, weakening the attack. An associated problem is the need to correct for atmospheric distortion of the beam which disrupts the phase front and weakens it further. Taken together, these problems present significant obstacles to using lasers to do much more than burn out a satellite's sensors. On the other hand, the ability to build a laser as large as is necessary to generate the required amount of power, and the lack of size constraints in building sophisticated devices to keep the beam aimed and focused, suggest a potential for effective ground-based laser weapons.[104] In any case it seems prudent to invest in more ground-based laser *research* before initiating the costly process of modifying these weapons for use in space.

The type of ASAT favored by the United States has been, and is currently, the direct ascent ASAT. Direct ascent ASATs are characterized by the fact that they do not actually enter orbit, but attempt to loft a device into the path of an oncoming satellite.

Rocketdyne, 1997; on-line, Internet, March 29 1998, available from http://www.fas.org/spp/military/program/asat/brief9711/index.html.]
[104] It should be noted that airborne lasers could also be used in the ASAT role. Such an approach would yield increased mobility and avoid firing the laser through most of the atmosphere. However, drawbacks such as drastically reduced power availability and

Due to the speeds involved, these devices have been likened to shooting a bullet at a bullet. In general, the ASAT is launched into the path of a satellite from a location on or near the satellite ground-track, and shortly before the target satellite arrives overhead. The kill mechanism is the kinetic energy inherent in the velocity differential between the vertically ascending ASAT and the orbiting satellite. With a velocity differential of about 17,500 mph for a low orbiting satellite, a direct hit will assure destruction.

While the United States has pursued several antisatellite programs in the past, only one has actually intercepted an orbiting satellite.[105] This ASAT was an air-launched system comprised of an F-15 fighter aircraft and a two-stage missile. The first stage motor of the missile was a modified short-range attack missile (SRAM), and the second stage an Altair motor. The 17 ft-long missile was to loft a miniature homing vehicle weighing about 15 kg into the path of a target satellite, whereupon it would make the final corrections needed for a direct impact.[106] The system was successfully tested against a satellite on September 13, 1985.[107] The program was cancelled in 1988 when congress voted to continue a two-year-old ban on further tests against objects in space.[108]

Another direct ascent ASAT is under development in the United States today. The Army's KE ASAT program is a ground-based two-stage missile that delivers a "kill vehicle" into the path of the target satellite. Launched by a derivative of the Minuteman booster, the kill vehicle optically tracks the target satellite and deploys a sail-like debris mitigation device shortly before impact. While the capability of the system is classified,

---

limitations on laser size are such that this concept seems questionable, at least with current technology.

[105] The United States developed several ASAT systems in the 1960s, including Program 505 Nike-Zeus, Program 437 Thor, and SAINT. The first two were direct ascent systems using nuclear weapons as the kill mechanism. While both were successfully tested with simulated warheads, neither actually destroyed a target satellite. The SAINT system was to be a co-orbital device to inspect, and if necessary destroy, enemy satellites. Technical problems forced termination of the program before any flights were actually made. [Curtis Peebles, *Battle for Space*, (New York: Beaufort Books, 1983), 820-101.]

[106] "USAF Vehicle Designed for Satellite Attack," *Aviation Week & Space Technology*, January 14 1985, 21.

[107] The target satellite was an Air Force test program satellite 11.3 ft., long, 6.8 ft in diameter, and weighing 1,936 lb. It was in a 320 NM polar orbit with an inclination of 97.7 degrees. ["Defense Dept. Plans Next Test Firing of Air-Launched ASAT System," *Aviation Week & Space Technology*, September 23 1985, 20.]

it is claimed that a single launch site will be able to "reach any satellite in low earth orbit."[109] Considering its much more powerful booster, the KE ASAT will probably be effective against satellites in orbits much higher than the 320 NM demonstrated by the air-launched ASAT.

An alternative approach to an anti-satellite weapon is to match orbits with the target satellite and destroy it with an explosion in close proximity. The Soviet Union built and tested such a system during the 1970s and '80s. The Soviet designs placed the ASAT in an orbit that was similar to that of the target satellite and intercepted the target in one or two orbits. The system used either radar or infrared/optical sensors to home in on the target and exploded into a swarm of pellets when it came within range. Of the two sensors used, the infrared/optical system failed in every test while the radar system was successful 64 percent of the time. As with the direct ascent systems discussed above, the Soviet system was limited to satellites in LEO, although the demonstrated maximum altitude was considerably higher at 1,710 km.[110]

Another potential co-orbital ASAT could be a derivative of the device to control uncooperative satellites mentioned above. Obviously if a satellite can attach itself to an uncooperative target in order to maneuver it into a more favorable orbit, then it can just as easily attach itself and explode. While destroying a satellite will leave little doubt as to which nation was responsible, particularly during a war, such an approach would produce much more definitive results. In terms of practicality, using such a device against high altitude orbits could prove to be more costly than is necessary.

If it becomes necessary to attack satellites that do not descend to low altitudes (hundreds to possibly several thousand kilometers), direct ascent attacks will probably be

---

[108] The political resistance to tests against orbital targets along with large cost overruns combined to persuade the Air Force to cancel the program. [Eric J. Lerner, "ASAT nears the end," *Aerospace America*, February 1988, 9.]

[109] "Kinetic Energy Anti-Satellite Program (KE ASAT) Background and Overview," slide briefing by Rockwell Corp and Rocketdyne, 1997; on-line, Internet, 29 March 1998, available from http://www.fas.org/spp/military/program/asat/brief9711/index.html. One point not mentioned in the slide briefing is that the kill vehicle uses a visible light tracking system that may require daylight attacks. ["KE ASAT hover test is highly successful," August 12 1997; on-line, Internet, 7 February 1998 available from http://www.fas.org/MhonArc/BMDList_archive/msg00249.html.]

[110] Richard L. Garwin, Kurt Gottfried and Donald L. Hafner, "Antisatellite Weapons," *Scientific American* 250, no. 6, June 1984, 47-9.

unfeasible. As the target satellite's orbital altitude increases, the size of the booster needed to reach it must also increase. Eventually the booster required becomes too large to be practical. A better method is to place an ASAT into a more efficient transfer orbit and then deploy a small attack vehicle when it nears the target. While this would not be a co-orbital intercept, expending resources on a co-orbital weapon is probably not necessary. The closing velocities between a satellite in a transfer orbit and the target satellite would be small enough to make the final tracking and closing maneuvers much simpler than those of a direct ascent ASAT.[111] No nation is currently developing such a system (at least publicly), but the ability to do so is inherent in the technology required to place a satellite in high earth orbit and many countries have this capability.[112] Given sufficient incentive, developing an antisatellite weapon capable of reaching geosynchronous satellites should be only a moderately challenging technological effort for a spacefaring nation.

Regardless of whether a co-orbital or direct ascent ASAT is considered, ground-based weapons have inherent advantages over their space-based counterparts. Given a wisely selected launch site, ground-based weapons have the ability to attack satellites in virtually any orbital inclination. Air- or sea-launched weapons would have a similar capability. This inherent flexibility would allow fewer ground-based than space-based weapons to provide a similar amount of capability.

While it will take one ASAT to destroy one satellite regardless of where the ASAT is based, space-based ASATs are even more limited in that they will probably only be capable of destroying one *particular* satellite. For a space-based ASAT to destroy an enemy satellite, it must be deployed in an orbit that will permit it to intercept its target with the propellant available on board. If the ASAT is to be kept reasonably small, then it

---

[111] Whereas intercepting a satellite in LEO requires systems capable of handling velocity differentials on the order of 8 km/s, the velocity differential between a transfer orbit and a satellite in GEO is only about 1.4 km/s.

[112] The nations currently able to place satellites in geosynchronous orbit include the United States, Russia, Ukraine, Japan, China and France. The other members of the European Space Agency (ESA) also have access to GEO, but political ramifications may make launching weapons somewhat problematic. In addition, India is considered to be close to having the capability to launch satellites into GEO. [Phillip Clark, ed., *Jane's Space Directory*, (Jane's Information Group Limited, Sentinel House, Coulsdon, England: 1997).]

will probably be limited to engaging satellites that are in similar orbits. In most circumstances this lack of maneuverability will limit the ASAT to being able to attack only a few targets, often only one. If the enemy is unknown, then enough ASATs must be deployed to engage all probable targets. A ground-based system would avoid such limitations. If the launch site is located on the equator, then an ASAT will be able to engage satellites in any orbital plane. With the addition of larger boosters and orbital transfer vehicles, satellites in the highest orbits could also be attacked.

The responsiveness of ground-based weapons would also be nearly as good as that of their space-based counterparts. With the possible exception of the space-mine, intercepting a satellite with a satellite will often take as long or longer than intercepting it from the ground. The nature of orbital dynamics is such that the time necessary to achieve the orbital geometry required for a space-to-space intercept will often be as long as waiting for an optimum launch opportunity from the ground. Ground-based weapons have the additional advantage of being accessible for maintenance and modifications, should they be necessary.

It is also probable that ground-based weapons would cost less than their space-based counterparts. Although both systems would require boosters of about the same size,[113] what would make a space-based system more expensive is the additional complexity needed for a weapon to survive months or years in orbit and then perform flawlessly. Ground-based weapons, on the other hand, could be stored in climate-controlled buildings or silos until they were needed.

Preventing Launch of Adversaries' Space-Based Assets

The potential for using a ballistic missile defense system to deny an enemy access to space was discussed in Chapter 2. While using a pre-existing BMD system for this purpose may be feasible, the costs of doing so must be weighed against those of using other assets. An effective BMD system would be capable of reaching across hundreds of miles to intercept a ballistic missile within seconds of its launch. Space-based weapons

---

[113] Since the energy needed to reach a given satellite is the same regardless of when it is expended, both ground- and space-based systems would require boosters of about the same size.

capable of accomplishing such a mission will not be cheap. Expending these expensive-to-replace weapons against an ascending satellite booster does not appear to be the most cost-effective approach to space control. More importantly, creating such a system just to perform a job that could be more easily accomplished by conventional weapons would be even less prudent.

Virtually all space launches are made from fixed locations that are well known. All of these sites are within the range of either stealth aircraft or cruise missiles. The facilities needed to prepare the satellites and boosters for launch are highly vulnerable, especially during the days prior to a launch when the vehicle is positioned on the launch pad. In this position the satellite and booster are little more than a large bomb being readied for a carefully controlled detonation. Since the status of an upcoming launch is readily evident to U.S. airborne or satellite reconnaissance, timing an attack to take advantage of this most vulnerable condition is relatively easy. A conventional attack on such a target will not only destroy the particular satellite, it will most likely cause severe damage to the launch complex and prevent or delay subsequent launches as well.

To mitigate this vulnerability a potential foe could choose to create mobile launch systems. The sea-launch system being developed by an international consortium will be such a system and will provide the capability to launch from virtually anywhere on the world's oceans.[114] However, it will also be quite vulnerable since it employs very large, slow-moving vessels. A number of platforms, from attack submarines to land-based bombers could destroy these vessels with little difficulty. Air-launched systems would present a more difficult target, but current systems are only capable of launching the smallest satellites into the lowest orbits. If it became necessary to deny an enemy even this limited capability, then attacks against the airfields from which the systems operate would be little different from attacks against any other militarily significant airfield and could be carried out using other methods.

---

[114] The Sea Launch system is a joint venture between Boeing, the Norwegian ship builder Kvaerner, and Russian and Ukrainian aerospace firms RSC-Evergia and NPO-Yuzhnoye. The system employs a moveable oil rig as a launch platform and has a specially built ship that transports a pre-prepared rocket out to the rig for launch. [Mark Ward, "Business in Space," *Inside Science*, (supplement within *New Scientist*), May 24 1997, 4.]

An often-cited problem with the idea of attacking satellite launch facilities is the possibility that political considerations will place these facilities off-limits. Whether this is because a third party is launching an adversary's satellites or that such attacks would be deemed too escalatory, attacking launch facilities may not be possible. However, potential restraints on the use of force in a particular scenario do not necessarily mean that developing and deploying a boost-phase intercept system is a good idea. If developed, the ground-based ASATs mentioned above should be more than adequate for denying an enemy access to space-based assets. In light of these alternatives, the billions of dollars needed to create a space-based system to attack satellites during their boost phase could be better spent in other areas.[115]

Conclusions

As illustrated in the previous chapter, space-based weapons have the potential to perform the space control mission, but only with high costs and high technological risk. Ground-based weapons also have the potential to meet the requirements of the space control mission. What is more, they offer similar capabilities at potentially lower cost and appear to have more flexibility. Tables 1 and 2 provide a comparison of the relative strengths of the various systems in terms of some key measures. Some may question the need for any kind of space control weapons, but if they are deemed necessary, the best options appear to be ground-based launch-on-demand weapons.

Table 1. Space-Based Weapons for Space Control

	Response Time	Technical Risk	Reliability	Vulnerability to Attack	Verifiability of Effects	Cost
SBL	Very Good	Extremely High	???	High	Good	Very High
Space Mines	Excellent	High	Fair	Medium	Very Good	High

---

[115] While a system designed merely for launch suppression may not need to be as capable as a BMD system, an estimate of the cost may be the Global Protection Against Limited Strike system (GPALS), envisioned to stop a small ballistic missile attack, and projected to cost $46 Billion. ["Sounding Taps for Star Wars and the Stealth Bomber," *The Defense Monitor* XX, no. 5, 1991, 2.]

KE	Good	High	Fair	High	Excellent	High
Co-Orbital	Good	High	Fair	High	Very Good	High
KE Launch Suppression	Very Good	Very High	???	High	Excellent	Very High

Table 2. Ground-based Options for Space Control

	Response Time	Technical Risk	Reliability	Vulnerability to Attack	Verifiability	Cost
Non-Destructive Measures						
Coerce Providers	???	None	Unknown	N/A	Poor	Low
Jamming Satellites	Good	Low	Med-High	Low	Poor	Low
Blinding Satellites	Good	Low	Med-High	Low	Poor	Low
Attack Ground Stations	Good	Low	High	Low	Very Good	Medium
Interfere with Enemy Satellites	Good	Medium	Medium	Low	Excellent (positive feedback)	Medium-High
KE Weapons						
Army KE ASAT	Good	Medium	High	Low	Excellent	Med-High
F-15/ ASAT	Good	Medium	High	Low	Excellent	Med-High
Co-Orbital Attacks						
Ground to LEO	Good	Medium	High	Low	Very Good	Med-High
Ground to HEO	Good	Medium	High	Low	Good	Med-High

67

Chapter 4

Attacking Terrestrial Targets: Ground-Based Alternatives for Force Application

...a sword of Damocles [to] hang over the heads of the imperialists when they decide the question whether or not to unleash war.

Nikita Krushchev
Pravda, December 9, 1961

Possibly the most controversial types of space-based weapons are those designed to attack targets on the ground or in the air. The idea of having weapons orbiting overhead, awaiting a signal to begin raining down upon whomever the United States determines to be an enemy is alarming to many nations. Because of the political costs of deploying such weapons, the United States should only build them if there are compelling advantages to be gained from doing so. The two main categories of orbital force application weapons currently being considered for development are those for ballistic missile defense and attacking surface targets. Airborne targets that remain within the atmosphere are extremely difficult to attack directly, and will only be discussed in passing. The primary purpose of this chapter is to compare the potential capabilities of orbital bombardment, space-based ballistic missile defense, and space based RF weapons with those of their terrestrial counterparts.

Lasers will receive only brief attention in this chapter for the simple reason that they are virtually ineffective against surface targets and have the potential to attack only the highest flying airborne targets. Due to a combination of atmospheric absorption and the limited amount of power available once in orbit, lasers operating on known principles are incapable of delivering significant amounts of power against ground targets. Even if a space-based laser could generate 25 megawatts, the amount needed for an effective space-based BMD system, it would be of little use against ground targets, which are much more robustly built. More relevant to the force application mission are weapons that operate on the better understood principles of physical impact.

Alternatives to Orbital Bombardment

The various proposals for space-based force application weapons were discussed in detail in Chapter 2. Before any of these concepts are actively pursued, it is necessary to determine if there are alternatives that can perform the same missions. After a brief review of the orbital weapons, this chapter will evaluate which systems already in the inventory can accomplish these missions. Finally, launch-on-demand concepts will be reviewed to evaluate what potential they may have for meeting the same needs.

Orbital bombardment weapons can theoretically attack any point on the surface of the earth with little or no warning. The surprise nature of these attacks, the defender's virtual inability to counter an attack from space once it has been launched, and attributes such as high impact velocities have been the traditional reasons for advocating orbital bombardment weapons.[116] A careful analysis of these claims, and the difficulties inherent in attempting to capitalize on them, indicates that they have shortcomings that make conventional weapons superior.

As outlined in Chapter 2, orbital bombardment weapons have significant inherent drawbacks. Achieving the greatest impact velocities (10 to 11 km/s) requires high altitude orbits from which the time needed to hit a target is on the order of hours even under optimum conditions.[117] This relatively long time tends to detract from the surprise nature claimed for orbital weapons, while the increased velocities are of comparatively little value. Weapons delivered low earth orbit would have better response times and

---

[116] Ivan Bekey, "Force Projection from Space," *New World Vistas, Air and Space Power for the 21st Century, Space Applications Volume*, (Washington D.C.: USAF Scientific Advisory Board, 1995), xviii, 83-84.
[117] To attain velocities in the 10 to 11 km/s range, satellites must be in orbits with an altitude of more than 40,000 km. The transfer time from a 40,000km orbit to impacting the earth's surface is about 5 hours, and would yield an impact velocity of about 10 km/s. The time to hit a target on the earth would probably be longer since it is unlikely that the weapon would be in the proper position to initiate an immediate attack.

their impact velocities on the order of 4 to 5 km/s are more than adequate, but they would be more vulnerable to enemy attack.

Another drawback of orbital weapons, at least for the near future, is that impact velocities of more than 1.5 km/s are of little use. The materials available for constructing penetrating warheads are inadequate to withstand greater impact velocities and penetrate into deeply buried hard targets. Eroding rods, on the other hand, are limited by the fact that they only penetrate 2 to 3 times their own length into the ground and hence are also unable to penetrate deeply buried targets. These drawbacks are quite significant, since they imply that orbital bombardment weapons have serious limitations, at least for the foreseeable future.[118]

Provided they can be precisely located, deeply buried hardened structures comprise a hitherto invulnerable target set against which orbital bombardment weapons may be effective. These targets are constructed hundreds of feet below the surface. If new materials that are only now being investigated prove to be as good as expected,[119] it will be possible to destroy such targets with orbital weapons. In contrast, current conventional weapons are unable to affect targets buried more than 50 to 60 feet beneath the surface.[120]

When deciding to attack hardened targets, it is worthwhile to consider just exactly what is important enough to protect so carefully. During, WWII these targets ranged from Adolf Hitler's bunker in Berlin to underground weapons factories used to build V-2 rockets. More recently, hardened targets have included command and control facilities such as Cheyenne Mountain, the U.S. underground command and control center in Colorado, and the various bunkers used by Iraq to protect command and communication nodes. The advent of precision weapons has made burying some of these types of facilities ineffective. For instance if a nation were to place its weapons factories in

---

[118] Joseph A. Smith, Advanced Concepts Engineer, Laurence Livermore Laboratories, interview with the author 11 February 1998.

[119] New materials called "Nanolaminates" have the potential to withstand impact velocities of up to 14,000 ft/s (4.3 km/s). [Joseph A. Smith, Advanced Concepts Engineer, Laurence Livermore Laboratories, interview with the author 11 February 1998.]

[120] Mark Hewish, "Adding new punch to cruise missiles," *Jane's International Defense Review* no. 31, January 31 1998, 41-2.

underground bunkers today, it would be fairly easy to strike the entrances and exits every few days to prevent raw materials from being taken in and finished products from being delivered to the field. Recent technological developments may also lead to a reduced need to place communication nodes underground. As communication networks transition from landlines to satellite systems, the ground links may become as small as a hand-held telephone.[121] With the added impetus of orbital bombardment weapons continually passing overhead, nations and corporations alike might decide to make their communication systems completely independent of vulnerable ground nodes.

The countermeasures available to an opponent also need to be considered before a new weapon system is developed. If a facility is dear enough to a nation then it is possible to make it virtually immune to attack, even from orbital weapons. Reinforced concrete has been the material of choice for constructing underground bunkers. However, to protect truly important assets, it is better to bore deep into solid granite. Granite is more than three times as strong as reinforced concrete against a projectile travelling at 1 km/s, and is still almost 20 percent stronger if hit at 4 km/s.[122] While it is much more difficult to bore into solid granite than it is to dig a hole, build a concrete bunker, and then bury it, if something is important enough, then extreme measures may well be taken to ensure its protection. If a target is placed deep enough into a granite massif, then even nuclear weapons will be unable to destroy it. Attempts to use orbital bombardment weapons against such a target would be equally futile.

If the high-value asset is at all portable, a much easier and less expensive method of protection may be to make it mobile. The 1991 Gulf War against Iraq showed how difficult it can be to find even relatively large vehicles, such as mobile Scud missile launchers, in a relatively barren desert environment.

---

[121] Motorola's Iridium system is an example of such a system. Iridium will allow people to make a phone call (or send a fax or connect to the internet) from anywhere in the world using only a small hand-held telephone. [John V. Evans, "New Satellites for Personal Communications," *Scientific American*, April 1998, 74,5.]

[122] Comparison is based on the stagnation pressure at the tip of a penetrating body, which is proportional to the maximum stress on the penetrator. Preston Carter, "HyperSoar, A Concept for Global Reach - Global Power," Lawrence Livermore National Laboratory. Briefing to the author on January 15 1998.

Some targets are too large to make mobile and do not merit the heroic measure of tunneling kilometers into granite. These targets are the ones for which orbital weapons would be best suited, but most of them can also be attacked by conventional weapons ranging from artillery to long-range bombers. The weapon needed to attack a particular target will depend on factors such as the needed promptness of the response and how well the target is defended. While no single conventional weapon has the range and hitting power theoretically available with orbital weapons, a variety of conventional weapons can destroy almost all of the targets that would be vulnerable to orbital bombardment. In addition, most of the targets that can only be attacked from space will be equally vulnerable to sub-orbital weapons.

If space-based weapons are to be used to attack targets other than deeply buried hard targets; their suitability is even more questionable. As discussed in Chapter 2, the Common Aero Vehicle is a concept that could be employed as a space-based weapon. The GPS-guided CAV would be a maneuvering reentry vehicle with considerable cross-range capability. It would provide a means for dispensing submunitions from orbital weapons to make them effective against a more diverse array of targets. The submunitions which have been proposed would be able to engage maneuvering targets, both airborne and surface, as well as area targets. However, these kinds of targets are even more vulnerable to conventional weapons than are hard targets.

Conventional Missiles

Conventional missiles are able to attack and destroy many of the same targets that orbital weapons would be used against. For some targets, short-range ballistic missiles such as the Army Tactical Missile System (ATACMS) could be used. Designed to dispense various types of submunitions, these ground-launched missiles are most effective against area targets such as armored or infantry formations. Improvements being undertaken to make this system effective against hard targets will add to these capabilities.[123] Their relatively short ranges, on the order of hundreds of kilometers, also limit the use of these missiles to the vicinity of the ground battle.

Air- and sea-launched cruise missiles are another alternative to orbital weapons. With ranges up to 1,300 km for non-nuclear missiles, and ranges of 2,500 km for nuclear-tipped versions, these vehicles already have the ability to destroy many of the targets suggested for orbital weapons.[124] Initially designed with the limitations of the SALT II arms limitation treaty in mind,[125] current cruise missile designs are somewhat limited in range and some targets deep within enemy territory may be beyond their reach. Newer missiles should be better, with the Advanced Cruise Missile reported to have a range of 3,000 km.[126] Since these missiles are basically small, autonomous aircraft, further extensions of their range would be relatively straightforward. Even with today's limitations, cruise missiles carried on either aircraft, submarines or ships have the ability to hit most important targets.

Originally intended for nuclear strike, cruise missiles have been modified to dispense submunitions against up to four separate targets apiece.[127] Aside from a somewhat limited range, the main shortcoming of cruise missiles is their limited capability against hardened targets. This weakness is now being addressed by the development of new warheads. With currently deployed warheads, a typical cruise missile has the ability penetrate approximately four meters of reinforced concrete. This makes them effective against many hardened surface targets, such as aircraft shelters, and even some underground installations. New warhead designs have the potential to

---

[123] Block 3 ATACMS missiles will carry a hard target penetrating warhead. [Duncan Lennox, ed., *Jane's Strategic Weapon Systems*, (Jane's Information Group Limited, Sentinel House, Coulsdon, England: 1997), Issue 26, January 1998.]

[124] Duncan Lennox, ed., *Jane's Strategic Weapon Systems*, (Jane's Information Group Limited, Sentinel House, Coulsdon, England: 1997), Issue 26, January 1998.

[125] While SALT II, which remains unratified, did not limit the ranges of air-launched cruise missiles, ground- and sea-launched cruise missiles could be tested up to ranges of 2,500 km, but could not be deployed. The fact that deployed sea-launched cruise missiles have a range of 2,500 km argues that the treaty is being ignored. [Kenneth P. Werrell, *The Evolution of the Cruise Missile*, (Maxwell AFB, AL: Air University Press, 1985), 175-6.   Duncan Lennox, ed., *Jane's Strategic Weapon Systems*, (Jane's Information Group Limited, Sentinel House, Coulsdon, England: 1997), Issue 26 January 1998.]

[126] Duncan Lennox, ed., *Jane's Strategic Weapon Systems*, (Jane's Information Group Limited, Sentinel House, Coulsdon, England: 1997), Issue 26 January 1998.

penetrate 6 to 9 meters of compacted soil and then still penetrate 3.6 to 5.5 meters of concrete. While this capability is still less than that of orbital bombardment weapons, this improvement threatens all but the most deeply buried targets.[128]

Another disadvantage of cruise missiles when compared with orbital bombardment weapons is their responsiveness. If sufficient numbers are deployed, orbital weapons should be able to hit a target anywhere on earth within a matter of hours.[129] In contrast, unless a submarine is in the region or the target is within range of pre-positioned aircraft, most missiles will generally not be available for at least a day or two. In most cases this should be adequate, but better responsiveness can still be attained without having to resort to orbital weapons.

Problems with cruise missile responsiveness and penetration capability could be overcome by using intercontinental ballistic missiles that are modified to carry non-nuclear KE weapons. ICBM-launched KE weapons would not be able to strike at the 11 km/s of some orbital concepts, but the 5 km/s they are able to achieve is still more than current penetrating warheads are able to withstand. This makes ICBMs equal to orbital weapons in hitting power, at least until materials technology advances dramatically.

Unfortunately, using ICBMs to deliver KE weapons has many problematic drawbacks, not the least of which is accuracy. ICBMs have been made very accurate over the years, but accuracy good enough for nuclear weapons is inadequate for precision weapons aimed at hardened targets. Improving the accuracy of the missiles will face the same problems as orbital weapons; the speeds of re-entry into the atmosphere (5-6 km/s) make communicating with a warhead virtually impossible.[130] Absent an inertial

[127] Ibid., RGM/UGM 109 Tomahawk.

[128] Mark Hewish, "Adding new punch to cruise missiles," *Jane's International Defense Review* no. 31, January 31 1998, 41-2.

[129] Approximately 36 satellites placed in 90-minute orbits could strike targets anywhere on the earth within about 45 minutes provided they had the ability to maneuver 1000 km from orbital track during descent. These maneuvers would reduce their impact velocity by a significant amount. More satellites or longer permissible wait times would alleviate this problem.

[130] As mentioned in Chapter 2, at speeds in excess of about 4.6 km/s the plasma surrounding a reentry vehicle prevents it from being able to transmit or receive singals. [W. Williamson et. al., "Technical Analysis of a Contingency Conventional Surgical Strike System," (Albuquerque, NM: Sandia National Laboratories, June 1995), 42. (Secret) Information extracted is unclassified.]

navigation system that is sufficiently accurate, destroying deeply buried hard targets will be difficult.

Until technology catches up, the CAV may be able to solve the problem of giving ICBMs a conventional attack capability. Since the CAV concept evolved from research into maneuverable ballistic missile re-entry vehicles, launching them with ICBMs is inherently feasible. The ICBM/CAV combination could provide the United States with a conventional global strike capability that is just as responsive as the current nuclear strike capability. This, however, may be its greatest flaw.

The main drawback for using ICBMs to deliver conventional weapons, either KE weapons or CAVs, may be the rather heavy nuclear baggage associated with them. Regardless of what they carried, ICBM launches would look exactly like a nuclear attack. While this aspect may be minimized by constructing new launch sites, necessary since launches made from current silos drop expended booster stages on the United States and Canada, even using alternate launch sites would probably cause anxiety among less-than friendly countries. Assurances from the United States regarding the nature of the warheads and their intended targets may be enough to prevent third-party nations from launching back, but the potential for escalation could exist.

Manned Bombers

Manned aircraft also have the ability to destroy most of the targets suggested for orbital weapons. Fighter and bomber aircraft have long been used against the array of targets for which the CAV is designed, and now have the ability to drop precision weapons that can penetrate many hardened structures. With global range, B-52 or B-1 bombers can carry cruise missiles to launch points within range of most targets that are of interest. Increased range for cruise missiles would bring virtually all targets within range of the bomber/cruise missile combination.

Manned bombers also have the potential to use ordnance that would overcome some of the shortcomings of cruise missiles with respect to hard targets. Rocket assist for bombs designed to penetrate hard targets has been demonstrated to increase their penetration capability. The rocket accelerates the bomb to a velocity of about 1.2 km/s, far less than orbital weapons, but still sufficient to penetrate over 15 meters of concrete.[131] Virtually all aircraft capable of dropping laser-guided bombs can carry these weapons, but high threat environments will necessitate the use of stealth assets.

Stealth technology gives the B-2 the ability to strike anywhere on the globe, including areas with a robust anti-aircraft defense, with a very low probability of being intercepted. The B-2 is already in the inventory, will be able to carry precision weapons like the Joint Direct Attack Munition (JDAM), and can strike virtually all targets currently outside the range of cruise missiles. Rocket assist and penetrating warheads are being investigated for use with JDAM and would give the B-2 a striking power close to that of orbital weapons.

A disadvantage of manned bombers, including the B-2, is their response time. Strikes against the most remote targets will require the pre-positioning of aerial refueling aircraft so that the bombers will be within range. This pre-positioning combined with the relatively low speed of aircraft will generally slow response time to days rather than hours. The need for support aircraft and the crews to fly them also add considerably to the *cost* of delivering a strike. However the hardware costs have largely been paid once the aircraft have been acquired, and the operations, maintenance and personnel costs pale in comparison to the expense of fielding a truly robust orbital bombardment system.

Another potential drawback to manned bombers is the possible loss of effectiveness for stealth technology in the not-too-distant future. Were this to occur, many targets currently vulnerable would become less accessible. Orbital weapons offer the ability to strike these targets regardless of what happens to the effectiveness of stealth. On the other hand, improvements to cruise missiles also have the potential to make these targets vulnerable, and at much lower cost.

Transatmospheric Vehicles

For attacking targets that are not vulnerable to conventional aircraft or missiles, launch-on-demand transatmospheric vehicles (TAVs) have the potential to provide the same capabilities as orbital weapons. TAVs are envisioned as reusable vehicles that are able to place payloads in orbit, or to deliver them anywhere in the world in a matter of

---

[131] Hewish, 42.

hours. TAVs could be either manned or unmanned, with unmanned TAVs being the most feasible in the near to mid-term. Most TAV concepts are expected to land like aircraft and will either take off like aircraft or will be launched from other aircraft. TAVs are also expected to have much shorter turnaround times between missions than current space-lifters, with aircraft-like operations being the ultimate goal.[132]

In essence, TAVs are merely a concept for providing low-cost, responsive space-lift. The most promising concepts for TAVs are those launched from carrier aircraft, since using existing heavy lift aircraft significantly reduces the cost of the first stage.[133] A drawback to these designs is that they are limited in size by the capacity of the carrier. With military satellites gradually getting smaller, this limitation may not be very significant. In fact, the military Technical Requirements Document for TAVs specifies a desired payload size of 1000 lbs, well within the capability of air-launched designs.[134] While ground-launched single-stage-to-orbit (SSTO) vehicles may prove better for launching medium or heavy payloads, they are not likely to be as responsive as smaller air-launched two-stage-to-orbit (TSTO) vehicles. SSTO vehicles are also likely to be much more expensive to design and build, and will probably not be available as soon.[135]

The ability to deliver payloads from space on short notice makes TAVs an obvious alternative to space-based weapons. Although they would be space weapons in some respects, the fact that weapons delivered by TAVs would not be launched until needed would make them less controversial than permanent orbital platforms. Yet since TAVs would be travelling at orbital speeds, they could deliver weapons with the same hitting power as space-based weapons, but with less controversy and at lower cost.

---

[132] For a detailed discussion of the potential capabilities of TAVs and other re-useable launch vehicles see Michael A. Rampino, "Concepts of Operations for a Reusable Launch Vehicle," (Maxwell AFB, AL: School of Advanced Airpower Studies, June 1997).
[133] When used to launch TAVs, carrier aircraft are essentially the first stage of a two-stage-to-orbit (TSTO) booster. This allows the TAV landing gear to be designed to support only landing loads, rather than the much greater fully fueled take-off weight. Using modified commercial aircraft as carriers allows the use of proven designs and greatly lowers development costs. [Daniel Gonzales et al., *Proceedings of the RAND Project AIR FORCE Workshop on Transatmospheric Vehicles*, RAND Report MR-890-AF (Santa Monica, Calif.: RAND, 1997), 31-40.]
[134] Daniel Gonzales et al., 13-14.
[135] Mel Eisman, Daniel Gonzales, *Life Cycle Cost Assessments for Military Transatmospheric Vehicles*, RAND Report MR-893-AF, (Santa Monica, Calif.: RAND, 1997), 30-1.

An alternative to orbital TAVs is a sub-orbital concept called HyperSoar that has been suggested by Preston Carter of the Lawrence Livermore National Laboratory. A HyperSoar vehicle would not actually attain orbit, but would fly a profile that skipped in and out of the atmosphere. Combined-cycle engines, which operate as either air-breathing engines or rockets depending on the phase of flight, would power the aircraft. The flight profile of skipping in and out of the atmosphere has the advantage over hypersonic flight within the atmosphere of allowing the aircraft's skin to cool during the time spent outside of the atmosphere. This concept has the advantage over orbital TAVs of not requiring the "ΔV" necessary to achieve orbit, and hence it requires less powerful engines and uses less fuel. A HyperSoar vehicle could also be used as the carrier aircraft of a TSTO system, with the benefit of drastically reducing the performance requirements of the second stage vehicle. [136]

Using a HyperSoar-type vehicle to deliver KE weapons has the potential to be as effective as placing them in orbit. Traveling at Mach 10 (3 km/s), weapons dropped by a HyperSoar vehicle would need rocket assist to achieve velocities equal to those of orbital weapon, but unless the materials improvements discussed earlier are made, 1.5 km/s is as fast as is currently useful. If rocket assistance is used, far less of it will be required than would be needed for weapons dropped from subsonic aircraft like the B-2. Hypersonic speeds, high altitude flight profiles, and their launch-on-demand operations would make these vehicles even less vulnerable than either orbital weapons or stealth aircraft. Thus orbital and sub-orbital TAV concepts have the potential to provide KE weapon capabilities identical to those of orbital weapons.

TAVs are just one of the concepts available for delivering weapons at orbital velocities without actually basing weapons in space. Expendable boosters such as the Pegasus XL built by Orbital Sciences Corp. could also provide this capability. While life

---

[136] A potential problem for the HyperSoar concept is that the combined cycle engine concept has yet to be proven feasible. [Preston Carter, "HyperSoar, a concept for Global Reach - Global Power," Lawrence Livermore National Laboratory. Briefing to the author on January 15 1998.]

cycle cost analyses indicate that reusable TAVs would be considerably cheaper,[137] Pegasus is a proven booster and meets many of the requirements for a launch-on-demand system to deliver weapons at orbital velocities. Specifically, the Pegasus XL has a responsiveness of about 15 days and can lift an 1100 lb payload into LEO.[138] Weapons like the CAV could be designed to make use of this booster, but would be quite expensive to use, as launching a Pegasus typically costs about $14 million.[139] While this might be feasible for a "silver bullet" weapon to be used against the highest priority targets, it would be cost-prohibitive as a major part of the force structure.

If it is deemed necessary to have a global multi-mission strike capability, this need could be met by a system like the CAV coupled with either sub-orbital launch vehicles such as ICBMs, expendable boosters such as Pegasus, or reusable TAVs. Considering the problems with ICBMs mentioned above, the other launch vehicles would probably be better alternatives, with TAV concepts appearing to be the least expensive for long-term operations.

Whether used for precision strikes against deeply buried hard targets or to dispense area-type weapons, expendable or re-useable launch vehicles are viable alternatives to space-based weapons. If placed on alert, each of the systems described above could deliver KE weapons almost as quickly as those placed in orbit. Launch-on-demand systems would be as difficult to intercept as orbital weapons, and would arguably be more difficult to attack before launch, than would space-based weapons waiting in orbit. While launch-on-demand KE weapons face most of the same technological hurdles as do orbital KE weapons, they are likely to be much less controversial.

It may be possible to develop and deploy an orbital bombardment system at less cost than equivalent launch-on-demand systems, since the latter systems require the development of a new class of lift vehicle, but a responsive orbital system would have to be designed to withstand years of storage or be periodically visited for maintenance,

---

[137] Mel Eisman, Daniel Gonzales, *Life Cycle Cost Assessments for Military Transatmospheric Vehicles*, RAND Report MR-893-AF, (Santa Monica, Calif.: RAND, 1997), 30,31.
[138] Daniel Gonzales et al. 15.
[139] *Forecast International/DMS, Spacy Systems Forecast*, April 1998, Tab: Space Vehicles, Section: Pegasus Winged Launch Vehicle, 1.

either of which entails considerable expense. While potentially more expensive to develop and deploy, a launch-on demand system would have as a by-product a responsive space-lift system that could be used to launch other payloads. A dedicated orbital bombardment system would provide no such benefit. If a responsive space-lift system were developed for other reasons, then the launch-on-demand system would be even cheaper. It can be argued that an orbital bombardment system could be made somewhat more responsive, but a launch-on-demand system would have virtually the same capability at potentially lower cost.

If delivered from conventional aircraft, none of the weapons discussed above, neither the KE weapons nor the types delivered by the CAV, are likely to engender any significant controversy. While weapons launched from these aircraft may not be effective against the deepest and hardest targets, one must question whether this small target set is worth the extremely high cost of developing and deploying a weapon system specifically designed to strike it. If the answer is yes, then sub-orbital weapons or launch-on-demand orbital weapons could do the same job at lower cost in terms of both dollars and controversy than their space-based equivalents.

Ballistic Missile Defense

The boost-phase engagement portion of ballistic missile defense is perhaps the only mission for which orbital weapons are uniquely suited. While space-based weapons have the potential to attack ballistic missiles before launch, these targets can also be attacked by conventional and stealth aircraft, as well ballistic and cruise missiles. If the missile launchers in question are mobile, then conventional aircraft are likely to be the only systems that can search out and destroy them. Space-based sensors may assist in this effort, but the flight times of orbital weapons are such that mobile missiles will be likely to have moved before the weapon arrives.[140] Autonomous submunitions that may be

---

[140] Barring extraordinary luck with orbital positioning, even a LEO system would have at about a 45-minute response at best. The Gulf War against Iraq showed that this is not fast enough, since mobile Scuds were launched and then re-positioned within about 10 minutes. [United States Department of Defense, *Conduct of the Persian Gulf War* (Washington D.C.: Department of Defense, 1992), 167.]

designed for hunting mobile missiles will favor neither space-based nor conventional systems since they will be deliverable by either.

Space-based weapons can also attack ballistic missiles after the boost phase, but a space-based system designed to attack missiles in the coast phase would probably have to be of a different design than one for boost-phase intercept. Lasers designed for boost phase intercept rely on the vulnerability of thin-skinned liquid fuel tanks under intense loads to provide the mode of destruction; the warhead bus or the warheads themselves are much more robust targets while they are coasting along. KE weapons designed to engage boost-phase ballistic missiles would also be poor choices for post-boost intercept. Due to differences in the equipment and software needed to detect, identify, and track individual warheads, significantly more capable interceptors would be needed for a boost-phase system to be effective against post-boost targets. While boost-phase weapons might be designed to attack both types of targets, their already high costs would undoubtedly increase further.[141] Orbital weapons are by no means uniquely suited to attack post-boost ballistic missiles. In fact the current national missile defense (NMD) program calls for post boost-phase intercepts to be conducted by ground-based upper and lower tier defenses.[142]

Attacking ballistic missiles during boost has a number of advantages. First of all, a ballistic missile is most vulnerable during this part of its trajectory. Tracking is simplified because the missile is easy to see due to its intense infrared signature. Successful attacks during this phase are the most effective since a missile during boost has not yet started deploying multiple warheads or decoys. A final advantage to boost-

---

[141] As discussed in Chapter 2, the Brilliant Pebbles orbital BMD system would probably have cost in excess of the projected $55 billion. [United States General Accounting Office, *Report to the Chairman, Legislation and National Security Subcommittee, Committee on Government Operations, House of Representatives: Strategic Defense Initiative, Need to Examine Concurrency in Development of Brilliant Pebbles*, GAO/NSIAD-91-154, (Washington, D.C.: General Accounting Office, March 1991), 6.]

[142] The Exoatmospheric Kill Vehicle (EKV) is a key part of the Ground-Based Interceptor (GBI) portion of the national missile defense system being developed by the Ballistic Missile Defense Organization (BMDO). The EKV is to acquire, track and destroy ballistic missiles during the midcourse phase of their trajectories. ["National Missile Defense Exoatmospheric Kill Vehicle," BMDO Fact Sheet 97-01, (Ballistic Missile Defense Organization, Washington D.C.: September 1997), 1.]

phase intercept is that the missile may fall back on the launching nation, and will at a minimum fall well short of its target.

The boost phase is probably the only phase for which orbital interceptors are uniquely suited. While some airborne concepts have been investigated or are being developed, all of these entail placing an aircraft fairly close to the launch site. The concept with the longest range is the airborne laser (ABL), which is calculated to have an effective range of several hundred kilometers against a Scud-type missile.[143] Ranges this short will make it nearly impossible to place the large, highly vulnerable aircraft needed to carry the lasers close enough to the launch sites of a major adversary to be effective. Concepts that envision air-launched missiles to perform the intercept suffer from similar problems.

While aircraft capable of carrying missiles to intercept ballistic missiles may be made stealthy enough to loiter in the vicinity of launch sites; these sites are likely to be too dispersed or mobile to allow a reasonable number of aircraft to keep all of them within range. The aircraft would also be vulnerable during daylight hours, providing an adversary with the simple option of launching during the day. Regardless of whether an air-launched boost-phase interceptor uses lasers or missiles, virtual air supremacy will be necessary if the aircraft are to be able to keep launch sites within range.

There are alternatives other than orbital weapons to circumventing the need for air supremacy. It may be possible to develop cheap, high-altitude, long-endurance unmanned aircraft (UAVs) capable of engaging ascending ballistic missiles. These aircraft would need stealth characteristics allowing them to loiter for days over a region of known launch sites. They would also have to be inexpensive so that enough could be deployed that they would flood a region of suspected launch sites. When a ballistic missile is launched, the aircraft would launch high-velocity missiles designed to intercept ballistic missiles in the boost phase and bring them down. Both the UAVs and the missiles would need to be very sophisticated and would require considerable resources to develop and deploy. However it is probable that a system such as this would be no more expensive, and would be more technologically feasible, than a system which relies on orbital weapons.

---

[143] Geoffrey E. Forden, "The Airborne Laser," *IEEE Spectrum*, September 1997, 49.

If other concepts prove impractical, an orbital defense system may be the only viable method for boost-phase interception of ballistic missiles, but as outlined in Chapter 2, it will be a major technological challenge and very expensive. Vast numbers of satellites will be required to provide coverage against even a limited missile attack. Given the need to place these weapons in low earth orbits, they will also present lucrative targets for a ground-based ASAT system.

Setting aside technological and cost hurdles, the greatest barrier to deploying a space-based BMD system may well be treaty limitations. While most other types of non-nuclear space-based weapons are not prohibited by international treaties, the 1972 Anti-Ballistic Missile (ABM) treaty specifically prohibits space-based BMD systems. This treaty not only covers deploying orbital ABM weapons; it proscribes even testing the components of such a system.[144]

Given the political will to do so (an admittedly unlikely proposition considering domestic and international political opposition to the idea), the United States could unilaterally abrogate the ABM treaty. Unfortunately this abrogation would, by definition, occur during early testing of components of the system, long before any kind of useable weapons (even prototypes) have been built. If this abrogation is discovered, which would be virtually certain considering the kinds of tests that will be required,[145] other nations will take note and may start taking appropriate countermeasures. The most straightforward of these would be simply to deploy large numbers of missiles so as to overwhelm the system. Given the large disparity in cost between building missiles and deploying an orbital BMD system, building enough missiles to overwhelm the BMD

---

[144] Article 5 of the Anti-Ballistic Missile Treaty prohibits the field-testing of ABM systems and their components whether they are air, land, sea, or space based. [Pericles Gasparini Alves, *Prevention of an Arms Race in Outer Space: A Guide to the Discussions in the Conference on Disarmament*, UNIDIR/91/79, Annex A (United Nations, N.Y., United Nations Institute for Disarmament Research: 1991), 63,4.]

[145] In orbital testing of either a laser or missile interceptor against a ballistic missile, the locations of the missile test ranges will make it virtually impossible to keep the tests secret.

system should not be difficult, especially if decoy missiles were to be used.[146]   A potentially even more effective way to circumvent an orbital BMD system would be to produce long-range cruise missiles. Orbital weapons would be virtually useless against cruise missiles, and given their low technology and significantly lower cost,[147] many nations might opt to direct their energies toward procuring these weapons.

While it appears that orbital weapons are necessary if a BMD system is to have a boost-phase component, the benefit of an effective BMD system is itself questionable. The orbital components of such a system would not only suffer from the costs and difficulties outlined in Chapter 2, the deployment of such a system may well prompt the development of countermeasures and alternative weapons that would render a ballistic missile defense system irrelevant.

Radio Frequency Weapons

The orbital RF weapon is a concept that appears promising but has little hard evidence to support the claims being made for it. If forecast improvements in the technology of high power RF systems and antennas occur, orbital RF weapons could provide on-demand degradation or destruction of an enemy's electronic equipment, and jamming of his radar and communications. Provided the previously examined difficulties of controlling extremely large antennas in space are also overcome, a relatively small number of RF weapons placed in geosynchronous or Molniya orbits could provide global coverage. This capability would be available worldwide without the need to deploy aircraft and equipment or put American lives at risk.[148]

---

[146] Unguided, or only marginally guided, ballistic missiles which would be little more than rocket motors and fuel tanks would be considerably cheaper than the real thing. They would be orders of magnitude cheaper than the optimistically estimated $46 billion needed to provide the limited coverage of the GPALS system described in Chapter 2. ["Sounding Taps for Star Wars and the Stealth Bomber," *The Defense Monitor* XX, no. 5, 1991, 2.]

[147] Cruise missiles are much cheaper than ballistic missiles as well, with a BGM-109 Tomahawk cruise missile costing $1.1 million (in 1998 dollars), much less than the LGM-30G Minuteman III costing $4.2 million (in 1978 dollars). [*Forecast International/DMS Market Intelligence Reports: Missiles*, 1998, Tab: D, Sections: "AGM-109/BGM-109 Tomahawk," pg. 2, and "LGM-30F/LGM-30G Minuteman," pg. 1.]

[148] Bekey, 84-85.

While space-based RF weapons appear to have great potential, the needed technological developments will probably entail considerable cost. Moreover, manned aircraft can also jam radar and communications. Although since the U.S. Air Force has recently retired much of its jamming capability in the form of the EF-111, and Navy EA-6Bs will only be able to assume part of the EF-111's former role, more capability is arguably needed. If this is true, the question becomes one of how to best provide this capability.

As mentioned above, space-based RF weapons have the potential to do much more than jam radar and communications, which is the limit of airborne systems. Moreover, the space-based weapons would look much like large radio telescopes or other inoffensive equipment, making them much less controversial to deploy. However, spending the vast sums of money needed to develop and eventually deploy such a system seems questionable in an era of severely limited defense spending. Although, investments in this technology have the potential to yield huge dividends, much less investment would be needed to remedy any current shortfall in jamming capability. As with many decisions made during a period of austerity, the outcome will probably hinge more on the short-term needs of the warfighter than on the potential merits of orbital RF weapons.

Conclusion

From the foregoing discussion, it appears that the only missions for which space-based weapons are uniquely suited are those of boost-phase ballistic missile defense and possibly RF attack against enemy electronic equipment. The first of these has significant treaty implications and both are concepts that will require considerable time and resources to make them into viable weapons. A qualitative assessment of the merits of the weapons discussed in this chapter can be found in Tables 3 and 4. Whether or not these weapons are worth the time and effort will hinge on a number of factors, not the least of which are the international political implications of placing weapons in space.

Table 3. Space-Based Weapons for Force Application

	Response Time	Technical Risk	Reliability	Vulnerability to Attack	Verifiability of Effects	Cost
Orbital Attack						
KE	Excellent	Very High	???	High	Good	Very High
CAV	Excellent	High	???	High	Fair	Very High
BMD	Excellent	Very High	???	High	Good	Very High
RF	Excellent	Very High	???	Medium	Fair	Very High

Table 4. Ground-based Alternatives

	Response Time	Technical Risk	Reliability	Vulnerability to Attack	Verifiability of Effects	Cost
KE Attack						
Conv Missiles	Good	None	Generally Very Good	Low	Good	Low
Manned Stealth Bombers	Good	Low	Generally Very Good	Low	Very Good	Low
TAVs	Very Good	High	???	Very Low	Good	Very High
Other Attack						
Conv Missiles	Good	None	Generally Very Good	Low	Good	Low
Manned Stealth Bombers	Good	Low	Generally Very Good	Low	Very Good	Low
TAVs	Very Good	High	???	Very Low	Good	Very High
Airborne Jammers	Good	Low	Generally Very	Med	Fair	Med

			Good			

Chapter 5

Political Implications

By trying too quickly to arm itself for the future space battlefields, the United States could lose the very peaceful means of getting rid of a few thousands of enemy nuclear warheads without firing a single shot.

Pierre Lefevre
Le Soir, 22 October 1997

Deploying weapons in space could usher in a new era in warfare. While some say that this is inevitable, others maintain that space can and should be maintained as a weapon-free sanctuary. As suggested by the passage above, even a limited test against an orbiting satellite can spark international censure. The political repercussions of actually deploying weapons in space are likely to be much greater. If a decision to deploy orbital weapons is to be consciously made, and not merely the unthinking result of technical feasibility, then the political implications must be carefully weighed. While a thorough discussion of these implications is beyond the scope of this paper, the following overview should familiarize the reader with the most significant points.

Treaty Implications

Any deployment of orbital weapons would have to take into account current treaties regarding the use of space. The treaties of primary concern are the Charter of the United Nations (1945), the Partial Test-Ban Treaty (1963), the Outer Space Treaty (1967), the ABM Treaty (1972), the Environmental Modification Convention (1977), and the Moon Agreement (1979).[149] Taken together, these treaties and conventions prohibit placing nuclear or other weapons of mass destruction in orbit around the earth or the moon, prohibit placing military installations or weapons on the moon or other celestial bodies, and declare that space is to be used exclusively for "peaceful purposes."[150]

Aside from weapons of mass destruction, the treaty implications of deploying orbital weapons are somewhat vague. The preamble to the Outer Space Treaty of 1967 stipulates that space will only be used for "peaceful purposes." While peaceful purposes are never clearly defined in the treaty itself, the treaty incorporates by reference the Charter of the United Nations (UN), which defines peaceful purposes to include the inherent right of self-defense.[151] The vagueness with which "peaceful purposes" is defined has prompted considerable discussion of its meaning. Interpretations range from banning any type of weapon whatsoever, to permitting purely defensive weapons to be deployed. None of the proposed interpretations would permit the deployment of offensive weapons in space.[152]

The problem with attempts to limit space-based weapons to those that are defensive is that most space-based weapons—like most other weapons—are difficult to categorize. This fact has been noted by the UN Conference on Disarmament, which cites the dual ASAT/ABM capability of many defensive ABM concepts as making the systems potentially offensive.[153] This is mirrored by the potential dual capability of many ASAT concepts which, given their potential ABM capability, would be in violation of the 1972 ABM treaty. While some argue that the ABM treaty has outlived its usefulness and is in

---

[149] For a more thorough discussion of international and treaty issues relating to the military use of space, see Glen H. Reynolds and Rovert P. Merges, *Outer Space: Problems of Law and Policy*, 2nd ed. (Boulder: Westview, 1997), 48-134; or Philip D. O'Niell Jr., "The Development of International Law Governing the Military Use of Outer Space," in Durch, ed., *National Interests and the Military Use of Space* (Cambridge, MA.: Ballinger Publishing Co., 1984), 169-200.

[150] Pericles Gasparini Alves, *Prevention of an Arms Race in Outer Space: A Guide to the Discussions in the Conference on Disarmament*, UNIDIR/91/79, Annex A (United Nations, N.Y., United Nations Institute for Disarmament Research: 1991), 56-80 and Annexes A and C.

[151] Alves, 143.

[152] The UNIDIR publication cited above discusses the concept of "peaceful purposes" through out its length, but the primary arguments are laid out on pages 12 - 13. Alves, 12-13.

[153] Alves, 35.

fact no longer even valid,[154] the lack of a clear distinction between offensive and defensive orbital weapons makes any deployment controversial.

The ABM Treaty is the most restrictive treaty currently in force that bears on weaponizing space. This treaty limits the United States and the Soviet Union each to a single ground-based ABM site.[155] The treaty is unusual since it does not specify each type of system that is prohibited; instead it is written to prohibit everything and then lists exceptions, the one ground-based system permitted for each signatory. The effect of this structure is that new technologies that could be used as ABM weapons are automatically excluded. Interpreting the treaty has led to considerable controversy, such as the whether orbital mirrors used to aim ground-based lasers at satellites would be components of an ABM system. Since these mirrors could be used to aim the laser at a ballistic missile, many nations hold that they would be proscribed, regardless of the mission for which they were intended.[156] As long as it remains in force, the 1972 ABM Treaty will greatly complicate any attempt to place weapons in orbit.

International Reaction

The international political implications of space-based weapons are already evident. Speaking through the UN Secretariat of the Conference on Disarmament, many nations have raised concerns about the destabilizing effects of placing weapons in orbit.

---

[154] Senator Jon Kyl argues that since the Soviet Union dissolved, there is no longer a treaty. He led a Senate movement to block a memorandum of understanding designating Russia, Ukraine, Kazakhstan and Belarus as successors to the USSR and keep the treaty in force. Jon Kyl, "An Effective Antimissile Strategy," *The Wall Street Journal*, May 22 1997.
[155] Under current interpretation this is now Russia, Ukraine, Kazakhstan and Belarus.
[156] Duncan Lennox, ed., *Jane's Strategic Weapon Systems*, (Jane's Information Group Limited, Sentinel House, Coulsdon, England: 1997), Issue 26 January 1998.

The main concern centers on the possibility of an arms race in space.[157] Not only is the deployment of U.S. ASAT weapons likely to prompt other nations to try to match this capability, the deployment of even a limited BMD system could spark such a race, since most BMD concepts will also be able to perform the ASAT role. Had it been made to work, the most notable BMD concept, the "Brilliant Pebbles" portion of the former Strategic Defense Initiative (SDI), would not only have provided defense against a ballistic missile attack, it would have enabled the United States to virtually close off space access to the rest of the world. This would have been possible because the capability needed to stop even a limited missile attack is enough to prevent other nations from launching any satellites at all. While some might desire this kind of control, it is unlikely that the international community would willingly acquiesce to such a move.

Today, the United States is in the enviable position of being the only superpower to survive the Cold War. Many models of political interaction would predict that a nation with so much power would prompt other nations to form alliances against it.[158] The fact that this has not happened is arguably a result of past U.S. restraint in exercising power. For instance, during the Cold War the United States allowed the other North Atlantic Treaty Organization members much more say in the structure of the organization and its decision-making processes than was necessary given their dependence on the U.S. nuclear umbrella.[159] This reluctance to aggressively use military power to further U.S. interests has prompted other nations to trust that the United States will not abuse its military superiority. A unilateral move to put weapons in space could undermine this trust.

One example of options open to other nations responding to a unilateral weaponization of space on the part of the United States is especially worthy of note. This response would be for another nation to deploy non-stealth space mines near each orbiting U.S. weapon. Once these weapons were in place, the nation launching them would need only to explain what they were and the conditions under which they would be

---

[157] Alves, Part II.

[158] For thorough discussion of international alliances and "balancing" among nations see Stephen M. Walt, *Origins of Alliances*, (Ithaca New York: Cornell University Press, 1987). Chapter 5 of Michael W. Doyle's *Ways of War and Peace* also discusses the concept of "balancing" (New York: W.W. Norton & Company, 1997), 161-194.

used. These weapons would be relatively inexpensive to design and produce, and if parked next to a multi-billion-dollar space-based laser, could negate the utility of the laser.[160] Furthermore, if overt space mines were deployed in response to space-based weapons, it is almost certain that they would be placed near other U.S. military satellites as well.

In light of international opposition, unilaterally deploying weapons in space has little to recommend it. Such an offensive attitude (in both senses of the word) would do little to generate international support for actions such as the 1991 Gulf War. Some may argue that the United States' current position of power makes international support irrelevant and that the United States did not need a coalition to defeat Iraq, but the costs of acting unilaterally would undoubtedly have been much higher. It seems unwise to alienate potential allies at the same time that force reductions may make acting unilaterally difficult or impossible.

Domestic Resistance

As the first openly proposed plan for putting weapons in space, the Strategic Defense Initiative generated more controversy than any previous space weapon system. The arguments against SDI centered on three general areas: the strategic instability that would be generated by pursuing a nuclear advantage; the inherent infeasibility of the concepts being explored; and the projected expense of the programs. Taken together, these problems spelled the end of SDI. Those who thought that the program was technologically unfeasible and a waste of money were able to garner support from those

---

[159] John Lewis Gaddis, *We Now Know: Rethinking Cold War History*, (Oxford: Camden Press, 1997), 288-9.

[160] Although similar in many respects to the space mine concept discussed in Chapter 2, a non-stealth space mine would avoid the most problematic difficulties associated with one which must remain undetected. Specifically, two of the biggest constraints, size and power source, would be eliminated. Since a non-stealth space mine could be as big as necessary, it could carry ample propellant to carry out its mission and electrical power could be supplied by solar cells. Building such a space mine would present few, if any, significant technological challenges. All that would really be needed would be a moderately maneuverable spacecraft packed with explosives. The guidance and control system would be no more complex than that needed to rendezvous with another spacecraft, so such a weapon would be a relatively inexpensive to build and deploy.

who deemed a successful program to be politically destabilizing and likely to lead to nuclear holocaust. Regardless of the merits of the arguments, the domestic political resistance became such that SDI was eventually terminated.[161]

Tests of the F-15 ASAT system also generated domestic controversy. Some of the concerns verged on paranoia, such as using the weapons to destroy Soviets early warning satellites so that the United States could launch a preemptive nuclear strike.[162] Others thought ASATs should never be developed because using weapons in space is an intrinsically bad idea.[163] While neither of these arguments was decisive, they added to the political resistance against the program. The final demise of the successful F-15 ASAT system has been attributed to cost overruns and a Congressional ban on further testing against targets in space. The U.S. Air Force cancelled the program in March 1988, and turned over ground-based ASAT development to the Army.[164]

If the controversy surrounding a recent U.S. test-firing of a ground-based laser at a satellite is any indication, opposition to using weapons in space remains strong today. This opposition continues to be directed against all weapons intended to engage targets in space, regardless of where they are based. The test firing of the MIRACL laser against an orbiting satellite prompted at least three articles in the *New York Times* alone, much more than would normally be expected for feasibility tests of a potential future weapon. This time the arguments centered on the even more relevant point of exactly who had the most

---

[161] For a detailed discussion of the costs and implications of SDI, see Crockett L. Grabbe, *Space Weapons and the Strategic Defense Initiative*, (Ames, Iowa: Iowa State University Press, 1991), Charles L. Glaser, *Analyzing Strategic Nuclear Policy*, (Princeton, New Jersey: Princeton University Press, 1990), and Steven E. Miller and Stephen Van Evera, eds., *The Star Wars Controversy*, (Princeton, New Jersey: Princeton University Press, 1986).

[162] A commentary in *Science* opened with: "The United States is about to test an ASAT that has no obvious target except Soviet early-warning satellites." The article stipulates that the *real* reason the United States was developing the F-15 ASAT was not to target the low-altitude satellites as was advertised, but so that it could be upgraded to eliminate Soviet early warning satellites allowing the U.S. to conduct a pre-emptive nuclear strike. Coming from an ostensibly reputable magazine, this type of speculation was surprising, even for a commentary. R. Jeffrey Smith, "Antisatellite Weapon Sets Dangerous Course," *Science* 222, October 14 1983, 140-2.

[163] Charles A. Monfort, "ASATs: Star Wars on the Cheap," *Bulletin of the Atomic Scientists*, v. 45, Issue 3, April 1989, 10-13.

[164] Phillip Clark, ed., *Jane's Space Directory*, (Jane's Information Group Limited, Sentinel House, Coulsdon, England: 1997), 164.

to lose were a space weapons race to start.[165] The fact remains that using weapons in space is still extremely controversial, and actually placing weapons in space is certain to be more so.

Space as Sanctuary

Space has long been treated as something of a sanctuary and kept free of weapons, a situation that is somewhat curious given the intense competition in technology and arms between the United States and the Soviet Union during the Cold War. The reasons for this traditional sanctuary status are somewhat ambiguous, beginning with an initial inability to build practical weapons, and gradually becoming a situation in which both sides had more to lose from space-based weapons than they had to gain.[166]

As soon as the United States began using reconnaissance satellites to determine Soviet military strength, the Soviets used the UN to try to get them banned. Once the Soviets attained a similar capability, these initiatives tapered off. At that point, the early 1960s, both nations were actively developing antisatellite capabilities and focused their efforts on ground-based weapons using nuclear warheads. The choice of nuclear weapons was based mainly on the fact that the technology for non-nuclear antisatellite

[165] William J. Broad, "Military is Hoping to Test-Fire Laser Against Satellite," *New York Times,* Monday, 1 September 1997, A-1. John E. Pike, the director of space policy for the Federation of American Scientists, a group opposed to anti-satellite weapons, is quoted as saying that "Shooting a satellite is shooting ourselves in the foot," presumably because showing the world how to disable our own satellites would be counterproductive. Follow-up articles and editorials also condemned the test: Letter to the Editor by Eugene J. Carroll Jr., Deputy Director, Center for Defense Information, Washington, "Space Laser Test Sows Military Hubris," *New York Times,* Friday, 5 September 1997, A-34. William J. Broad, "The Air Force Aims to Test Its Space Destroyer," *New York Times,* Sunday, 7 September 1997, IV-2.

[166] A thorough discussion the space sanctuary argument may be found in David W. Ziegler, *Safe Heavens: Military Strategy and Space Sanctuary Thought,* (Maxwell AFB, Ala.: School of Advanced Airpower Studies, 1997) and Paul B. Stares, *The Militarization of Space, U.S. Policy, 1945-1984,* (Ithaca, New York: Cornell University Press, 1985). The impact of political decisions on the development of space weapons may be found in Walter A. McDougall, *...The Heavens and the Earth: A Political History of the Space Age,* (Baltimore: Johns Hopkins University Press, 1985), and R. Cargill Hall, "Origins of U.S. Space Policy: Eisenhower, Open Skies, and Freedom of Space," John M. Logsdon, ed., *Exploring the Unknown,* (Washington D.C.: Government Printing Office, 1995), Chapter 2.

weapons was too immature to make them viable in the near-term. Space-based ASATs were dismissed for many of the reasons outlined in Chapters 2 and 3.[167]

The latter stages of the Cold War brought about an apparent re-evaluation of the need for antisatellite weapons. The last Soviet ASAT test was on June 18, 1982, and during the early 1980's the Soviet Union submitted to the UN a number of draft treaties for controlling weapons in space.[168] The U.S. response to this initiative can be said to have been made by Congress in September 1985, shortly after the successful test of the F-15 ASAT. This response was in the form of moratorium on ASAT testing for one year, that would be renewed as long as the Soviets did not test any more ASATs of their own. The moratorium, which prohibited tests against objects in space, was allowed to lapse by a Republican-led congress in 1995.[169] The tacit agreement not to pursue further ASAT capability seems to have been the result of both nations' growing reliance on space-based assets combined with the difficulty inherent in fully protecting them.[170]

While the post-Cold War environment does not present the United States with potential opponents as powerful as the Soviet Union, U.S. dependence on space-based assets is greater than ever. Even in relatively small-scale contingencies, U.S. forces rely heavily on space-based intelligence, navigation and communications. Current initiatives promise to increase our reliance on them even further, and include building satellites to gather real-time targeting information about ground targets, much like the airborne Joint Surveillance Target Attack and Radar System (JSTARS) provides today.[171] As the search for invulnerability continues to move from aircraft to satellites, a space sanctuary strategy would benefit the United States now more than ever.

---

[167] In the early 1960s it was more technologically feasible, and cheaper, to build a direct ascent ASAT with a nuclear warhead than it was to develop a more sophisticated orbital rendezvous system. Curtis Peebles, *Battle for Space*, (New York, N.Y., Beaufort Books Inc.: 1983), 77.

[168] Richard L. Garwin, et al., "Antisatellite Weapons," *Scientific American*, 250 no. 6, June 1984, 45, 47.

[169] Broad, A-12.

[170] Related concerns have been voiced by many other nations and are discussed in detail in Alves.

[171] Barbara Starr, "U.S.team to work on new target-tracking satellite," *Jane's Defense Week* 29, issue 12, 7.

Regardless of whether a space sanctuary is a feasible goal, placing weapons in space will generate both domestic and international opposition. It is even possible that a unilateral move by the United States would generate so much ill will, that other nations would band together in opposition.[172] Even if this did not happen, the political implications of placing weapons in space would be high, and would have to be factored into any such decision. Given the limited advantages offered by space-based weapons, adverse political implications make developing them truly questionable.

---

[172] Again, for thorough discussion of international alliances and "balancing" among nations see Walt's, *Origins of Alliances*, or Doyle's *Ways of War and Peace.*

Bibliography

Abrahamson, James A., et al. "Open letter to President Clinton," 15 Jan 98. Included in The Center For Security Policy press release No. 98-P7, January 1998.

"Advanced Anti-Satellite System in Offing." *Rockets and Missiles*, Vol. 18, no. 22, 30 May 1966, 69-70.

"Air Force 2025 in detail: Part II AF worries that space mines may threaten future ops." *Military Space*, Vol. 13, No. 23, 11 November 1996, 7.

Alves, Pericles Gasparini. *Prevention of an Arms Race in Outer Space: A Guide to the Discussions in the Conference on Disarmament.* UNIDIR/91/79, Annex A. United Nations. N.Y.: United Nations Institute for Disarmament Research, 1991. Part II.

Anselmo, Joseph C. "Launchers See Nothing But Blue Skies Ahead." *Aviation Week & Space Technology*, April 7 1997, 41-2.

Anselmo, Joseph C. "New Funding Spurs Space Laser Efforts." *Aviation Week & Space Technology*, 14 October 1996, 67.

Anselmo, Joseph C. and Bruce A. Smith. "Cost Drives EELV." *Aviation Week and Space Technology*, January 6, 1997, 27.

"Ballistic Missile Defense Organization Fact Sheet 97-09." Ballistic Missile Defense Organization, The Pentagon, Washington D.C.

Bate, Roger R., Doanld D. Mueller and Jerry E. White. *Fundamentals of Astrodynamics.* New York: Dover Publications Inc., 1971.

Baucom, Donald R. *The Origins of SDI, 1944-1983.* Lawrence, Kansas: University Press of Kansas, 1992.

"Belgium: Star Wars Has Come Down To Earth." *Foreign Media Reaction Daily Digest.* USIA Office of Research and Media Reaction, US Information Agency, Washington, DC, 22 October 1997. On-line. Internet, April 26, 1998. Available from http://www.fas.org/spp/military/program/ASAT/971922-miracl-mr.htm.

Bethe, John and Richard Garwin. "Appendix A: New BMD Technologies." *Daedalus: Weapons in Space*, Vol. II 114 (Summer 1985).

Broad, William J. "Military is Hoping to Test-Fire Laser Against Satellite." *New York Times*, Monday, 1 September 1997.

Broad, William J. "The Air Force Aims to Test Its Space Destroyer," *New York Times*, Sunday, 7 September 1997.

Bruner, William W. III. "National Security Implications of Inexpensive Space Access." Master's thesis, School of Advanced Airpower Studies, Maxwell AFB, AL, June 1995.

Carroll, Eugene J. Jr., Deputy Director, Center for Defense Information, Washington, "Space Laser Test Sows Military Hubris," *New York Times*, Friday, 5 September 1997, Letter to the Editor.

Clark, Phillip, ed. *Jane's Space Directory*. Coulsdon, England: Jane's Information Group Limited, Sentinel House, 1997.

Cushman, J. "To Detect ICBM Launch, AF Seeks Invulnerable Warning Satellites." *Defense Week*, January 16, 1984, 1, 10-11.

Daehnick, Christian C. "Blueprints for the Future: Comparing National Security Space Architectures." Master's thesis, School of Advanced Airpower Studies, Maxwell AFB, AL, 1995.

Deen, Thalif . "UN protocol brings laser blinding ban into force." *Jane's Defense Weekly*, February 11, 1998, 6-7.

De Selding, Peter B and Andrew Lawler. "SPOT Halts Sales of Gulf Area Imagery." *Space News*, August 13-19, 1990, 3, 21.

"Defense Dept. Plans Next Test Firing of Air-Launched ASAT System." *Aviation Week & Space Technology*, September 23 1985, 20-1.

Dickman, Major General Robert. "The Evolution of Space Operations and Warfare." Address to AIAA Symposium, Huntsville. AL., September 23. 1997. On-line, Internet, 2 February 1998. Available from http://www.acq.osd.mil/space/architect/ spcweb.html.

Dooling, Dave. "Ballistic Missile Defense." *IEEE Spectrum*, September 1997, 50-9.

Dornheim, Michael A. "Vandenberg Launches Eight Satellites." *Aviation Week & Space Technology*, February 23 1998, 41.

Dornheim, Michael A. and Joseph C. Anselmo. "Complex Antenna Is Star of Mission 77." *Aviation Week & Space Technology*, May 27, 1996, 58-9.

Doyle, Michael W. *Ways of War and Peace*. New York, NY: W.W. Norton & Company, 1997. Chapter 5.

Eisman, Mel, and Daniel Gonzales. *Life Cycle Cost Assessments for Military Transatmospheric Vehicles*. RAND Report MR-893-AF. Santa Monica, Calif.: RAND, 1997.

Estes, General Howell M. III. Commander In Chief, North American Aerospace Defense Command and U.S. Space Command. Prepared statement before the Senate Armed Services Committee, Washington D.C., March 13, 1997.

Evans, John V. "New Satellites for Personal Communications." *Scientific American*, April 1998, 70-7.

"Fact Sheet, National Space Policy." Washington D.C.: The White House National Science and Technology Council, 1996.

Forden, Geoffrey E. "A Panoply of Lasers." *IEEE Spectrum*, September 1997, 42.

Forden, Geoffrey E. "COILed to Strike." *IEEE Spectrum*, September 1997, 46.

Forden, Geoffrey E. "The Airborne Laser." *IEEE Spectrum*, September 1997, 40-9.

Forecast International/DMS Market Intelligence Reports: Space Systems Forecast, April 1998. Tab: Space Vehicles, Section: "Pegasus Winged Launch Vehicle."

Forecast International/DMS Market Intelligence Reports: Missiles, 1998. Tab: D, Sections: "AGM-109/BGM-109 Tomahawk," and "LGM-30F/LGM-30G Minuteman."

Gaddis, John Lewis. *We Now Know: Rethinking Cold War History*. Oxford: Camden Press, 1997.

Garwin, Richard L., Kurt Gottfried and Donald L. Hafner. "Antisatellite Weapons." *Scientific American* 250, no. 6, June 1984, 45-55.

Garwin, Richard. "How Many Orbiting Lasers for Boost-Phase Intercept?" *Nature*, 315 (May 23, 1985), 286-290.

Gertz, Bill. "Shared satellite laser test weighed." *The Washington Times*, Friday January 2 1998, A1.

Glaser, Charles L. *Analyzing Strategic Nuclear Policy*. Princeton, New Jersey: Princeton University Press, 1990.

Gonzales, Daniel, et al. *Proceedings of the RAND Project AIR FORCE Workshop on Transatmospheric Vehicles*. RAND Report MR-890-AF. Santa Monica, Calif.: RAND, 1997.

Grabbe, Crockett L. *Space Weapons and the Strategic Defense Initiative*. Ames, Iowa: Iowa State University Press, 1991.

Gray, Colin S. *American Military Space Policy: Information Systems, Weapon Systems and Arms Control*. Cambridge, MA: Abt Books, 1982.

Grossman, Karl. "Nuclear Gamble." *The Progressive*, September 1997, 20-3.

Hall, R. Cargill. "Origins of U.S. Space Policy: Eisenhower, Open Skies, and Freedom of Space." John M. Logsdon, ed. *Exploring the Unknown*. Washington D.C.: Government Printing Office, 1995, Chapter 2.

Hewish, Mark. "Adding new punch to cruise missiles." *Jane's International Defense Review*, no. 31, January 31 1998, 40-5.

Horelick, Arnold L. and Myron Rush. *Strategic Power and Soviet Foreign Policy*. Chicago: The University of Chicago Press, 1965.

Jacky, Jonathan. "Throwing Stones at 'Brilliant Pebbles." *Technology Review*, 20 October 1989, 20-1, 76.

"KE ASAT hover test is highly successful." August 12 1997. On-line. Internet, February 7, 1998. Available from http://www.fas.org/MhonArc/BMDList_archive /msg00249.html.

"Kinetic Energy Anti-Satellite Program (KE ASAT) Background and Overview." Slide briefing by Rockwell Corp and Rocketdyne, 1997. On-line. Internet, March 29 1998. Available from http://www.fas.org/spp/military/program/asat/ brief9711/index.html.]

Kyl, Jon. "An Effective Antimissile Strategy." *The Wall Street Journal*, May 22 1997.

Lennox, Duncan, ed. *Jane's Strategic Weapon Systems*. Jane's Information Group Limited, Sentinel House, Coulsdon, England: 1997. Issue 26, January 1998.

Lerner, Eric J. "ASAT nears the end." *Aerospace America*, February 1988, 8-10.

London III, John R. *LEO on the Cheap*. Maxwell AFB, AL: Air University Press, 1994.

London, J. and H. Pike. "Fire In the Sky: U.S. Space Laser Development From 1968." Paper no. IAA-97-IAA.2.3.06. American Institute of Aeronautics and Astronautics, Inc.

Matthews, William. "DOD restructuring SDI to fit a changing world." *Air Force Times*, 25 February 1991.

McDougall, Walter A. *...The Heavens and the Earth: A Political History of the Space Age*. Baltimore: Johns Hopkins University Press, 1985.

McKinley, Cynthia A.S. "When the Enemy Has Our Eyes." Master's thesis, School of Advanced Airpower Studies, Maxwell AFB, AL, June 1995.

Miller, Steven E. and Stephen Van Evera, eds. *The Star Wars Controversy*. Princeton, New Jersey: Princeton University Press, 1986.

Monfort, Charles A. "ASATs: Star Wars on the Cheap." *Bulletin of the Atomic Scientists*, v. 45, Issue 3, April 1989, 10-13.

Moorman, General Thomas S. Jr. Vice Chief of Staff, USAF. "The Challenges of Space Beyond 2000." Remarks to the 75th Royal Australian Air Force Anniversary Airpower Conference, Canberra. Australia, June 14, 1996. On-line. Internet, 9 January 1998. Available from www.af.mil/news/speech/current/The_Challenges_of_Space_Bey.html

Muolo, Michael J. *Space Handbook, A War Fighter's Guide to Space, Volume One*. Maxwell AFB, Ala.: Air University Press, December 1993.

Muolo, Michael J. *Space Handbook: An Analyst's Guide, Volume Two*. Maxwell AFB, Ala.: Air University Press, December 1993.

"National Missile Defense Exoatmospheric Kill Vehicle." BMDO Fact Sheet 97-01. Ballistic Missile Defense Organization, Washington D.C.: September 1997.

Neufeld, Michael J. *The Rocket and the Reich, Peenemunde and the Coming of the Ballistic Missile Era*. New York, NY: The Free Press, 1995.

New World Vistas, Air and Space Power for the 21st Century, Space Applications Volume. Washington DC: USAF Scientific Advisory Board, 1995.

O'Niell, Philip D. Jr. "The Development of International Law Governing the Military Use of Outer Space." in Durch, ed. *National Interests and the Military Use of Space*. Cambridge, MA.: Ballinger Publishing Co., 1984.

Parks, W. Hays. "Memorandum of Law: Trauvaux Preparatoires and Legal Analysis of Blinding Laser Weapons Protocol." *The Army Lawyer*, June 1997, 33-41. DA-PAM 27-50-295.

Peebles, Curtis. *Battle for Space*. New York: Beaufort Books Inc., 1983.

Peebles, Curtis. *Guardians: Strategic Reconnaissance Satellites*. Novato CA: Presidio Press, 1987.

Pike, John. "Space Based Laser." *FAS Space Policy Project Special Weapons Monitor*. On-line. Internet, 7 February 1998. Available from http://www.fas.org/spp/starwars/program/SBL.htm.

Rampino, Michael A. *Concepts of Operations for a Reusable Launch Vehicle*. Maxwell AFB, AL: Air University Press, 1997.

Reynolds, Glen H. and Rovert P. Merges. *Outer Space: Problems of Law and Policy*, 2nd ed. Boulder: Westview, 1997.

Rustan, Pedro L. "Clementine Test Results." Unpublished research results. Ballistic Missile Defense Organization, The Pentagon, Washington DC: 31 October 1994.

Saunders, Renee. "Eosat Sees High Demand for Gulf Images." *Space News*, September 24-30, 1990, 3.

Siegman, Anthony E. *Lasers*. Mill Valley, CA: University Science Books.

Scott, William B. "USSC Prepares for Future Combat Missions in Space." *Aviation Week & Space Technology*, August, 5 1996, 51-2.

Smith, R. Jeffrey. " Antisatellite Weapon Sets Dangerous Course." *Science* 222, October 14 1983, 140-2.

"Sounding Taps for Star Wars and the Stealth Bomber." *The Defense Monitor,* XX, no. 5, 1991, 2.

Spiegel, Peter. "Free Launch?" *Forbes*, February 24 1997, 76-8.

Stamm, Michael R. "How Technology is Changing the Optimum Size of Satellites." Unpublished Research Paper, Phillips Laboratory, Kirtland AFB, NM, December 1994.

Stares, Paul B. *Space and National Security*. Washington D.C.: The Brookings Institution, 1987.

Stares, Paul B. *The Militarization of Space, U.S. Policy, 1945-1984*. Ithaca, New York: Cornell University Press, 1985.

Starr, Barbara. "US team to work on new target-tracking satellite." *Jane's Defense Week* 29, issue 12, 7.

Stine, G. Harry. "Opening the Spaceways." *Barron's*, May 19 1997, 62.

"Summary of The Center for Security Policy High-Level Roundtable Discussion of 'The Need for American Space Dominance'." Attachment to The Center for Security Policy press release No. 98-16P, January 23 1998. On-line. Internet, 28 January 1998. Available from www.security-policy.org/papers/98-P16at.html.

Thomson, Allen. "Satellite vulnerability: a post-Cold War issue?" *Space Policy*, February 1995, 19-30.

Tirman, John, ed. *The Fallacy of Star Wars*. New York, NY: Vintage Books, 1983.

"Topaz 2 Go-Ahead to Speed U.S. Thermionic Effort." *Aviation Week & Space Technology*, 6 April 1992, 28.

United States Department of Defense. *Conduct of the Persian Gulf War*. Washington D.C.: Department of Defense, 1992.

United States General Accounting Office, Report to Chairman, Committee on Armed Services, U.S. Senate: Strategic Defense Initiative, Estimates of Brilliant Pebbles' Effectiveness Are Based on Many Unproven Assumptions. GAO/NSIAD-92-91. Washington, D.C.: General Accounting Office, 1992.

United States General Accounting Office, Report to the Chairman, Legislation and National Security Subcommittee, Committee on Government Operations, House of Representatives: Strategic Defense Initiative, Need to Examine Concurrency in Development of Brilliant Pebbles. GAO/NSIAD-91-154. Washington, D.C.: General Accounting Office, March 1991.

"USAF Vehicle Designed for Satellite Attack." *Aviation Week & Space Technology*, January 14 1985, 21.

U.S. Naval Research Laboratory. *Moonglow*. Washington D.C.: Naval Research Laboratory, June 1994.

Walt, Stephen M. *Origins of Alliances*. Ithaca, New York: Cornell University Press, 1987.

Ward, Mark. "Business in Space." *Inside Science* (supplement within *New Scientist*), May 24 1997, 1-4.

Werrell, Kenneth P. *The Evolution of the Cruise Missile*. Maxwell AFB, AL: Air University Press, 1985.

Widnall, Sheila E., Secretary of the Air Force. "The Space and Air Force of the Next Century." Presented at the National Security Forum. Maxwell Air Force Base AL., May 29, 1997. On-line. Internet, 9 January 1998. Available from www.af.mil/news/speech/current/The_Space_and_Air_Force_of_.html

Williamson, W., et. al. "Technical Analysis of a Contingency Conventional Surgical Strike System." Albuquerque, NM: Sandia National Laboratories, June 1995. (Secret). Information extracted is unclassified.

Ziegler, David W. *Safe Heavens: Military Strategy and Space Sanctuary Thought.* Maxwell AFB. AL: Air University Press, June 1997.

www.ingramcontent.com/pod-product-compliance
Lightning Source LLC
Chambersburg PA
CBHW081224280526
45787CB00006B/2511